D1591743

CHARACTER BUILDERS

Positive Attitudes and Peacemaking for Primary Children

A Program to Enhance Positive Attitudes
and Peacemaking Skills
Pre-School through Third Grade

SPARKY

Dr. Michele Borba

J

Jalmar Press

Character Builders: Positive Attitudes and Peacemaking for Primary Children
Copyright © 2001 by Michele Borba, Ed.D.

Jalmar Press
Permission's Department
P. O. Box 1185
Torrance, CA 90505
(310) 816-3085 fax: (310) 816-3092 e-mail: jalmar@worldnet.att.net
Website: www.jalmarpress.com

Published by Jalmar Press

Character Builders: Positive Attitudes and Peacemaking for Primary Children
A Program to Enhance Positive Attitudes and Peacemaking Skills
Pre-School through Third Grade

Author: Dr. Michele Borba
Editor and Story Writer: Marie Conte
Project Director: Jeanne Iler
Cover Design and Composition: Jeanne Iler
Interior Illustrations: Bob Burchett

Manufactured in the United States of America

10 9 8 7 6 5 4 3 2 1
ISBN: 1-880396-59-9

 # Contents

Contents

3 Deflecting Negative Comments

4 Accepting Compliments

5 Using I Messages to Solve Conflicts

Contents

Introduction

Building Character in Students

It's great to be great, but it's greater to be human.
—LUCY M. MONTGOMERY

In **my** consulting tours of school sites one experience became all too common. I'd walk into a classroom and notice a rule chart clearly posted with pre-established student expectations. Then I'd quietly walk up to a student, and choose one of the rules to quiz him on the meaning. The conversation generally went like this: "One of the rules on the chart says you are to act respectfully at this school. What does respect mean?" All too frequently the student's response would be a "shrug of the shoulders" or a simple "I don't know." I'd prod the student a bit further: "But it says you're supposed to act respectfully. Can you tell me what that looks like and sounds like?" "I don't know," the student would say.

What I just described is an all too common trend. Far too many of today's students do not know the meaning, behavior, and value of some of the most critical traits of solid character. And, there's a significant reason why: character traits, like skills, are learned. One of the primary ways students acquire these traits is by watching others do them right. Reflect on that statement a minute and ask yourself: "Who are my students watching to learn these traits?" Over the past few years we've witnessed a breakdown of appropriate role models for today's youth. Some of the primary sources that used to nurture the character of our students have broken down: the home, the neighborhood block, community support agencies, even the schools have become larger and less personalized. Role models for today's students are frankly atrocious. I watch in horror as a professional baseball player on national television is allowed to spit in an umpire's face and not be held accountable. I'm astounded when rock stars and authors of some of the most hateful lyrics I've ever heard receive standing ovations. I'm amazed that so many actors (some without even a high school diploma) are given contracts that quadruple the salary of the President of the United States. The breakdown of appropriate role models for our youth is clearly an enormous educational handicap.

The breakdown of appropriate role models is certainly not the only reason for the decline in solid character development of our youth. Dr. Thomas Lickona cites ten troubling trends among youth in our society that point to an overall moral decline. Over the past decades these ten indicators, which have been increasing significantly, show a failure of our students in the acquisition and development of character:

> "Sow an act, and you reap a habit. Sow a habit, and you reap a character. Sow a character, and you reap a destiny."
>
> —Charles Reade

Youth Trends and Moral Decline

1. Violence and vandalism.

2. Stealing.

3. Cheating.

4. Disrespect for authority.

5. Peer cruelty.

6. Bigotry.

7. Bad language.

8. Sexual precocity and abuse.

9. Increasing self-centeredness and declining civic responsibility.

10. Self-destructiveness.

Dr. Thomas Lickona: Educating for Character. Bantam: 1991. p. 16-18.

What can help turn these trends around? A recent poll revealed that 86% of adults surveyed believed that the number one purpose of public schools, apart from providing a basic education, is "to prepare students to be responsible citizens" (*Learning,* March/April 1997, page 3).

The truth is that school may well be the last beacon of hope for many of our students. How else will they have a chance to understand the value of traits called "responsibility" or "caring" or "respect" or "peacemaking" or "cooperation?" How else will these youths have the opportunity to watch someone model the trait appropriately? How else but at school will many of our students be able to learn these core skills they will need to succeed in every arena of their lives? Your power in your role of "educator" is extraordinary. The simple but profound truth is: How else but from a caring, committed teacher will many of today's students have a chance to expand their personal, social, and academic potential? This series, called *Character Builders,* will show you how.

Character Builders is purposely designed to be used in many ways. Each Character Builder can be infused into almost any subject. The themes have been carefully chosen based not only on research in character development but also in self-esteem theory. Each Character

Builder teaches students not only the trait but also a few core skills that will optimize their chances of success not only in school but also in life. The dream of educators is to have students who are more responsible, respectful, cooperative, peaceable and caring. Where do you begin? The key to enhancing student character development I believe is found in three critical premises. Above all else, keep these three premises in mind:

Premises of Character Development

- Character traits are learned.

- Character traits are changeable.

- Educators are able to create the conditions that enhance such change because they can control the learning environment and their attitude.

Let's analyze each one of these premises. Each one is important to understand if we want to enhance the character development of our students:

Character traits are learned. To the best of my scientific knowledge there are no genes for character development and self-esteem; none of our students are born with strong character. Instead, our children have acquired their character and self-esteem through repeated experiences in their pasts. Too often, the critical skills that enhance the core Character Builders have not been modeled or emphasized for students. You can make a difference for your students by deliberately modeling the traits and by providing them with opportunities to learn these skills.

"Show me the man you honor, and I will know what kind of man you are."

—Thomas Carlyle

Character traits are changeable. From the premise that character development is learned, a second principle arises naturally and unavoidably: If character traits are learned, therefore we can teach them and change them. It is essential to keep this concept in mind because it means that educators and parents do have tremendous power to teach critical skills and traits that optimize students' chances of success not only now but for the rest of their lives.

Educators are able to create the conditions that enhance such change because they can control the environment and their attitude. If character traits and skills are learned and changeable, then educators have the ability to create those changes by means of their attitudes, their curriculum content and the atmosphere they create. What is needed is the knowledge of what skills are most important to enhance each trait and which traits we should deliberately accentuate and model to help students "catch" the attitudes. That's what *Character Builders* is all about . . . and we haven't a moment to lose!

Character Builders is based on the same premises as *Esteem Builders: A K-8 Curriculum for Improving Student Achievement, Behavior and School Climate* that I published in 1989. The esteem-building series includes manuals for school, home, staff and workshop training, all designed to provide a comprehensive approach to developing high self-esteem in students. *Character Builders* is the next step in teaching students the skills that will help them succeed. The five core Character Builders complement the Esteem Builders for high self-esteem, namely: Security, Selfhood, Affiliation, Mission, and Competence. These five components serve as the foundation for enhancing students' positive self-perceptions, thereby encouraging the development of their potential and confidence in learning. The esteem building blocks have been sequenced within each character building theme to ensure that students will acquire these skills as well. It is strongly recommended that the themes within this manual be presented in the order in which they were written. This is the best way to ensure students' acquisition of the skills and character building traits. The five core Character Builders in this series are listed below along with their corresponding Esteem Builders.

Five Core Esteem and Character Builders

Esteem Builder Trait

Security
A feeling of comfort and safety; being able to trust others.

Selfhood
A feeling of individuality; acquiring an accurate and realistic self-description.

Affiliation
A feeling of belonging, acceptance or relatedness.

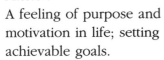
Mission
A feeling of purpose and motivation in life; setting achievable goals.

Social Competence
A feeling of success when relationships are handled respectfully and responsibly.

Character Builder Trait

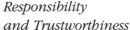
Responsibility and Trustworthiness
Doing what is right; being answerable and accountable to yourself and others.

Respect
Treating yourself and others in a courteous and considerate manner.

Cooperation and Fairness
Respectfully working with others in a fair and equitable manner to accomplish mutual goals.

Peaceability and Citizenship
Solving conflicts in a peaceful and responsible manner; building solid citizenship skills.

Caring
Showing concern and sensitivity for the needs and feelings of others; being compassionate and empathetic.

"We don't know who we are until we see what we can do."

—Martha Grimes

The activities in this book have been organized around six core universal moral values outlined by a group of twenty-nine youth leaders and educators at what has come to be known as the "Aspen Conference." The six core values are:

- Trustworthiness

- Respect

- Responsibility

- Justice and Fairness

- Caring

- Civic Virtue and Citizenship

Positive Attitudes and Peacemaking for Primary Children is written for younger students because we know the skills of positive attitudes and peacemaking are learned early in life. The sooner we can help children acquire positive character building traits and habits, the more likely these habits will be life long. The five additional books in the Character Builder series — *Responsibility, Respect, Cooperation and Fairness, Peaceability and Citizenship, and Caring* — are designed to enhance further development in character building. Though these books are designed for students in grades K-6, dozens of activities designed exclusively for young children are provided. In addition, each book presents new puppet characters which introduce the character themes of responsibility, respect, cooperation, peaceability and caring in meaningful and concrete ways to students.

FINAL THOUGHTS

*The chains of habit are too weak to be felt until
they are too strong to be broken.*

—Dr. Johnson

Social skills and character traits are most often acquired from watching others do them right. This very premise explains why so many of today's youth are underdeveloped in these traits and skills. With the breakdown of appropriate role models for today's students, it is imperative that educators deliberately exaggerate modeling the character trait and its behaviors at the school site. This is one of the easiest and certainly most important ways to show students the behaviors of character traits and skills. Never forget your own impact on your students. You may well be the only role model a student has to "see" what a Character Builder looks and sounds like.

Dozens of activities and ideas are suggested in this manual as ways for students to practice the skills for each Character Builder trait. Additional practice opportunities are provided by activities in *Esteem Builders: A K-8 Curriculum for Improving Student Achievement, Behavior and School Climate*. And, finally, further activities are offered for parents to reinforce the skills you present in the classroom in *Home Esteem Builders*.

The program is best when it is not a "tack on" new approach but instead infuses the skills and traits into the current curriculum. Before starting a new Character Builder theme, search through your textbooks and bookshelves for activities that naturally enhance the theme. Consider subjects such as literature, history, writing, art, science, math, physical education, music . . . every Character Builder has an endless potential of being integrated into your grade-level content. The theme will be not only more manageable for you but more meaningful for your students.

You will notice that while some of your students seem to understand the trait instantly, others need much more repetition and structured practice before they acquire the trait. If you notice some of your students have not grasped the concept, consider a few of these options:

A Model of the Trait. Many students need to "see" the trait and skills again (and again) in order to fully grasp the concept. One, two, or even three times may not be enough. Consider repeating your demonstration lesson with another student and then recreating a new T-chart with students who seem to need additional practice.

Trait Homework. Many teachers involve the parents as partners in character building. Students are required not only to practice the skills and traits at school but also at home. The more practice (particularly in a safe and supportive environment) the greater the likelihood the student will acquire the skill.

"Permanent" Safe Partners. Consider providing students who need additional practice with a "permanent" partner who is not a classmate. The term "permanent" means for a longer duration. The length of such a partnership is up to your discretion but do recognize that students low in security and in social skills are more threatened by demonstrating the trait with a number of different partners. They can benefit from having a "safer" partner they feel more secure with over a longer time period. Safe partners might include a younger student at the school (for example, a student in the sixth grade will find practicing the skill with a second grader or even kindergartener safer than a same-age partner), or a volunteer (a college or high school student or a parent).

Suppose a visitor comes to your site for the first time. He randomly pulls a student aside and asks one question: "What does your teacher or school stand for?" or "What does your teacher think are important kinds of behaviors to do?" Would the student be able to verbalize the Character Builder as an important part of your site? The answer to this question

> "You can easily judge the character of a man by how he treats those who can do nothing for him."
>
> —James D. Miles

Call Jalmar Press at (800) 662-9662 for a descriptive brochure about *Character Builders* manuals.

xii

"Teach a child to choose the right path, and when he is older he will remain upon it."

—The Bible

can quickly assess just how successful you've been in teaching Character Builders to your students. If that student can describe the Character Builder, it means you've accentuated the trait well enough that your students can say it to others. Keep on reinforcing it. They'll "own" it soon, which will impact their lives now and forever.

THE BUILDING BLOCKS OF SELF-ESTEEM

The following building blocks, based on the five feelings found in students with high self-esteem, are the sequential esteem-building steps incorporated in the curriculum.

BUILDING BLOCK
(Acquired Feeling)

STEPS FOR CHARACTER BUILDER
(Adult Functions)

 SECURITY

A feeling of strong assuredness. Involves feeling comfortable and safe; knowing what is expected; being able to depend on individuals and situations; and comprehending rules and limits.

1. Build a trusting relationship.
2. Set reasonable limits and rules that are consistently enforced.
3. Create a positive and caring environment.

 SELFHOOD

A feeling of individuality. Acquiring self-knowledge, which includes an accurate and realistic self-description in terms of roles, attributes, and physical characteristics.

1. Reinforce more accurate self-descriptions.
2. Provide opportunities to discover major sources of influence on the self.
3. Build an awareness of unique qualities.
4. Enhance ability to identify and express emotions and attitudes.

 AFFILIATION

A feeling of belonging, acceptance or relatedness, particularly in relationships that are considered important. Feeling approved of, appreciated and respected by others.

1. Promote inclusion and acceptance within the group.
2. Provide opportunities to discover interests, capabilities, and backgrounds of others.
3. Increase awareness of and skills in friendship making.
4. Encourage peer aproval and support.

 MISSION

A feeling of purpose and motivation in life. Self-empowerment through setting realistic and achievable goals and being willing to take responsibility for the consequences of one's decisions.

1. Enhance ability to make decisions, seek alternatives, and identify consequences.
2. Aid in charting present and past academic and behavioral performances.
3. Teach the steps to successful goal-setting.

 COMPETENCE

A feeling of success and accomplishment in things regarded as important or valuable. Aware of strengths and able to accept weaknesses.

1. Provide opportunities to increase awareness of individual competencies and strengths.
2. Teach how to record and evaluate progress.
3. Provide feedback on how to accept weaknesses and profit from mistakes.
4. Teach the importance of self-praise for accomplishments.

 1

How to Build Character

STEP 1: Focus on the Character Builder

STEP 2: Describe the Need, Value, and Meaning of the Trait

STEP 3: Teach What the Trait Looks Like and Sounds Like

STEP 4: Provide Structured Practice of the Trait

STEP 5: Give Immediate Feedback

How to Build Character

The unfortunate thing about this world is that good habits are so much easier to give up than bad ones.
—W. SOMERSET MAUGHAM

The lessons from *Positive Attitudes and Peacemaking for Primary Children* are especially valuable for today's youth. So many of our students today are lacking in critical character skills to help them cope and succeed in school as well as in life. These skills we once assumed were being taught at home. We can no longer make that assumption since, in many cases, they obviously are not. It is essential then to make sure that as educators we address such skills within our schools to help prepare our students for the twenty-first century.

While the four skills presented in this program are essential to character enhancement, they are by no means all the principles that could be learned on the subject. I strongly recommend that you continually review the skills (increasing positive attitudes, deflecting negative attitudes, accepting compliments, and reducing conflicts) often with your students. Children learn through repetition and modeling. We also know that our students require different amounts of time to learn. I urge you to also teach your students the essential skills of peacemaking, problem solving and decision making to further help them succeed in life.

Whether your efforts to enhance student character education are as a district, school, or individual, they are significant. The beauty of enhancing character is that it is contagious. Educators report over and over that though they began the effort singly, in no time others caught the spirit and joined forces. Their combined efforts have had a powerful effect. This is how we will turn the tide for countless students. Together, as teachers, we can make a tremendous difference in the lives of our students. The journey is long—and change may not be visible at once—but how sweet the reward: the chance for a child to succeed (and in some cases, quite literally, survive). Whatever your position, if children are in your care,

I hope you will take the lessons in this book to heart. The activities, skills and stories will enhance two critical Character Builders—positive attitudes and peacemaking—in our youth, both now and for the rest of their lives. We haven't a moment to lose, so let's get started.

Key Objectives for Positive Attitudes and Peacemaking

- To enhance students' awareness of appropriate positive language and peaceful deeds.
- To increase students' social skills through the use of positive comments toward others.
- To defuse negative language and behaviors.
- To learn the three components of receiving compliments—making eye contact, smiling, and responding verbally with "thank you."
- To develop students' ability to praise themselves as well as others.
- To teach students the technique of using "I Messages" as an appropriate coping strategy for dealing with anger, frustration, and conflicts.
- To increase sensitivity to others' emotions and express a vocabulary of emotion.

How to Teach Positive Attitudes and Peacemaking

Positive Attitudes and Peacemaking for Primary Children was designed as a tool for educators to use in enhancing a peaceful and positive learning climate for their students. Such a climate is critical to the core character building traits—Responsibility, Respect, Peaceability, Cooperation, and Caring—and to the development of the first esteem builder, Security. The program presents four main skills on the themes of peacemaking and positive attitudes. These skills, developed sequentially, are listed below:

- Increasing Positive Comments and Peaceful Deeds

- Deflecting Negative Comments

- Accepting Compliments

- Using I Messages to Resolve Conflicts

Increasing Positive Comments and Peaceful Deeds

Deflecting Negative Comments

Accepting Compliments

Using I Messages to Resolve Conflicts

There are five main teaching elements in this book, which are used to enhance each character building skill:

1. Sparky (and in some cases, both Sparky and the teacher) introduces the lesson with a story;
2. A mini-poster illustrates the main point of the lesson for students;
3. Children are taught concrete skills to use in enhancing character;
4. Following the lesson, students participate in hands-on activities featuring structured role playing in order to experience, in a concrete way, the principles of each theme; and
5. Extension activities, such as children's literature selections, are suggested as follow-up ideas for additional practice using the skills.

Experiential Approach

Creating a peaceful and positive learning climate is a critical aspect of character building. Developmental learning theory clearly tells us that young children learn best through concrete experience. *Positive Attitudes and Peacemaking for Primary Children* was designed with this concept in mind. The program appeals to young children experientially: visual aids depict character building language; positive comments and I messages are modeled verbally through storytelling and group interaction; and hands-on activities provide direct sensory contact with the elements of a peaceful and positive learning environment. Each aspect of the program builds on the skills and attitudes learned in earlier activities and are reinforced through multiple learning channels so that children can better understand and remember important character building principles.

Learning is not a simple process of putting information into students and then having them "put it out." Rather, real learning takes place when children are given an opportunity to experience new information at a level they can understand. To help students learn the four character building skills presented, the program utilizes many approaches. These include:

• **Skill Builder Posters.** Each of the core Character Builder skills taught in this book is accompanied by a poster. The posters purposely have a minimum of printed words and include illustrations for young readers. Posters may be duplicated on light-colored construction or cardstock paper. It is strongly recommended that the posters be enlarged at a print shop or on a xerox machine and then hung in the classroom to remind students of the skill.

• **Puppets.** To make the Character Builder skills more meaningful for young children, each core skill is introduced by a puppet. The patterns and directions to make the puppets are included in the book. The puppets liven up the lessons, reinforce the skills and teach children the critical concepts needed to learn new character traits.

• **Stories.** Many of the lessons are accompanied by simple, fun stories told by the Character Builder puppets. The stories are easily found in the manual because the text has been gray toned.

• **Role Playing.** To help students practice the skills, role playing activities are provided. New habits take much practice before they are learned and owned. It is strongly recommended that children act out the skills in the secure setting of the classroom where their actions can be instantly reinforced or corrected.

• **Activities.** Dozens of meaningful activities are suggested to reinforce the four peacemaking and positive attitude skills. Many of the tasks include ready-to-duplicate forms, and all activities involve a minimum of materials and preparation.

• **Extension Activities.** Following many of the activities in this book you will find extension activities. These suggestions are simple ways to extend the lesson one more step, oftentimes integrating the activity into another curriculum.

• **Songs and Jingles.** Several of the activities are accompanied by simple jingles or songs. These are designed to reinforce the concepts through rhythm and music. It's just another modality to ensure mastery.

• **Children's Literature.** One of the best ways to introduce, extend or review Character Builder skills is through children's literature. Many quality books that reinforce the activity or skill are provided throughout the book. Read them together and enjoy.

The program is designed in a deliberate sequence. Each of the four character building skills in *Positive Attitudes and Peacemaking* is presented in a specific order with the intention that young children will eventually master the principles introduced in previous activities. It is strongly recommended that you do the activities in the suggested sequence for maximum learning of the skills. Children learn through repetition and modeling.

Learning theory tells us that it generally takes 21 days before a new behavior is acquired. We also know that our students require different amounts of time to learn. Use your professional instinct as to how long each skill should be presented, and don't be afraid to retell stories and repeat activities. Children love to "redo" and often learn more the second and third time around. Above all...have fun with the program.

STEPS TO BUILDING CHARACTER TRAITS

Though each of the five Character Builders in this program are unique and consist of distinct skills and behaviors, the steps to teaching each character trait (Responsibility, Respect, Cooperation, Peaceability, and Caring) are the same. The staff should utilize the same five steps in teaching each Character Builder in this series. Skipping any step will be detrimental to the students' acquisition of the concept. There's an old Chinese proverb which is quite appropriate to the learning process. It says: "If you cut too many corners, you end up going around in circles." Each step is important in helping students learn these five core Character Builders.

Character Skill Builder Teaching Steps

1. **TARGET:** Focus on the Character Builder for at least 21 days.

2. **DEFINE:** Describe the need, value, and meaning of the trait.

3. **SHOW:** Teach what the trait looks like and sounds like.

4. **DO:** Provide structured practice of the trait for 21 days.

5. **REINFORCE:** Give immediate feedback and encourage use in life.

STEP 1: TARGET

Focus on the Character Builder

The first step to teaching any new character trait, skill or behavior is to target the skill visually (and ideally orally) to students. The more students "see" the trait the more they recognize that "this must be important...there it is again." If Character Builders are being accentuated school-wide, it is important that the poster for each trait and skill be accentuated throughout the school site. Everyone at the school needs to be reminded of the character builder trait.

Quick Ways to Target a Character Builder

- Clearly announce to students what the targeted trait is and keep it posted.

- Keep the Character Builder trait or skill posted as long as possible. Many teachers add a new Character Builder poster to their walls every month or two.

- Tell students your expectations regarding the trait.

- Announce the trait over the loudspeaker or at least start each morning with a one-minute Character Builder announcement.

- If Character Builders are being accentuated school-wide, it is important that the poster for each trait or skill be accentuated throughout the school site. Everyone at the school needs to be reminded of the trait.

> "Whoever one is, and wherever one is, one is always in the wrong if one is rude."
>
> —Maurice Baring

Keeping the Focus on Character

There are dozens of ways to focus on character traits and skills. Below are listed some of the simplest as well as some of the most unique ways to accentuate a character trait.

- **Character Builder Poster.** Each Character Builder trait comes with an 8½" × 11" poster. Photocopy the poster on bright-colored paper and hang it on walls for all to see. The form in this book can be enlarged at a printer's to a 18" × 24" size. The Character Builder puppet can be enlarged to hang up as a visual reminder for younger children.

- **Character Builder Assembly.** Many sites implementing school-wide character themes introduce the trait at a school-wide assembly. At this occasion the staff describes why the trait is important, distributes the poster to students, and even presents a short skit or movie about the trait.

- **Screen Saver.** This one wins the prize for the "most unique way to accentuate a character trait." I saw it at a magnet school in computers and technology. Each day a staff or student member wrote a brief sentence describing a school rule, theme or learning message about the targeted Character Builder on the site's central screen saver. Whenever anyone at the school used a computer, the first thing they saw was the screen saver message accentuating the trait.

- **Campaign Posters.** Student-made posters are often the simplest way to accentuate a character trait. Students can draw the guidelines using material such as colored poster board, marking pens, and construction paper. Posters can also be computer-generated and printed on colored paper. However posters are made, be sure to hang them everywhere and anywhere on school and classroom walls.

- **Flag Pole Banner.** On visiting a middle school in Austin, Texas, I knew when I was in the parking lot what behaviors that staff was accentuating for their students. A banner made from an old white sheet hung on the flag pole. Imprinted with bold-colored permanent marking, the banner stated one word: "EFFORT!" Each month the staff selected a different trait, and a group of students volunteered to make and hang the banner.

- **Character Builder Announcements.** By using the school loud speaker system, students can be orally reminded of the character traits and skills. Many schools use the first and last minute of each school day for Character Builder reminders. Principals can announce names of students "caught demonstrating the trait." Students can describe ways to appropriately demonstrate the traits or behaviors.

- **Character Builder Theme Songs.** A unique way to accentuate each Character Builder is by selecting a "theme song" to match each character trait. Play it over the loud speaker before the bell rings and during lunch. For example, the song from the television show, "Cheers," is a great way to accentuate the trait of Cooperation. There is no better song for the trait of Respect than Aretha Franklin's tune by the same name, "Respect."

STEP 2: DEFINE
Describe the Need, Value and Meaning of the Trait

The second step to teaching a new character trait or behavior is to convey to students exactly what the trait means and why it is important to learn. Though the trait may be targeted in the classroom and on dozens of posters throughout the campus, never assume students understand what the trait means. The trait should always be explained to students so that they can understand the concept within their knowledge base and experience. Though each Character Builder poster has a carefully constructed definition, keep in mind a definition generated by the students will be even more powerful. Here are a few other ways to define new traits and behaviors to students.

Quick Ways to Define a Character Builder

- Tell students specifically why they should learn the skill.
- Clearly explain the value of learning the trait.
- Specifically define the trait to students. "This is what I mean when I say the word caring...."
- Keep the definition posted in your classroom and, ideally, all around the school.
- Use your own personal examples to make the definition concrete.
- Find literature selections that define the trait.
- Ask students to clip news articles of events or people demonstrating the theme.

Below are many powerful suggestions of specific ways you can define a Character Builder for your students:

- **Define in Teachable Moments.** Use teachable moments to accentuate, define and model new behaviors to students. You might accentuate the behavior of "encouragement" by patting a student on the back and saying: "Keep it up. I know you can do it!" Take one more second to label and define the trait by saying, "Did you notice I just encouraged you?" Finally, define the behavior to the student in context by adding "…because I just patted you on the back and told you I knew you could do it." Many students need a moment to process the skill in context.

- **Label Traits as Students Use Them.** Whenever you see or hear a student displaying the targeted trait, take a moment to label it to the rest of the students. Point out specifically what the student did that demonstrated the trait and remember to be consistent in the use of terms. For instance, if "respect" is the term that appears on the Character Builder poster, use this same term to reinforce a student's behavior. Here are the steps to labeling a new behavior.

    1. *First, point out the behavior as soon as convenient with a label.*

        It is always best to point out the behavior the moment it happens so the student will be more likely to recall what he or she did. Also, any other students who are near the reinforced student will also benefit from hearing "what was done right." Suppose you are reinforcing "respect." Stop and label the appropriate behavior to the student:

        "Alex, that was respectful…"

    2. *Second, tell the student specifically what they did that was appropriate.*

        Usually, you can begin with the word "because" and then confirm to the student exactly what he or she did that was "respectful."

        "…because you waited until I was finished
        talking before you spoke."

- **Tell the Trait's Benefits.** Skills and behaviors are more meaningful and relevant to students if they understand the benefit of learning the skill. Take a moment to say the name of the Character Builder or the skill and why it's important. For example, "This month we will be learning about the value of caring. It's such an important trait because it helps make the world a kinder and gentler place."

- **Share Personal Beliefs.** Students need to hear your convictions regarding the trait. Why do you personally feel the trait is important? If you are targeting the trait of "respect," you might tell students how adamant you feel about not talking negatively about yourself or others. For instance, you could say: "One of the things that bothers me most is when I hear someone saying something unkind about themselves or someone else. I know unkindness hurts. In this classroom it is not allowed." Show them with your own behavior how strongly you believe in what you say.

> "Good manners and soft words have brought many a difficult thing to pass."
>
> —Sir John Vanbrugh

"Politeness is
not always the
sign of wisdom,
but the want
of it always
leaves room
for the suspi-
cion of folly."
—Walter Savage
Landor

- **Student Reporters.** One of the easiest ways to demonstrate the need for the trait is to point out its value in context. Anytime someone displays the trait, take a moment to label the Character Builder to students. Suppose you are accentuating "caring." Ask students to begin looking for others demonstrating the trait at the school. These students can assume the role of "reporters." Their job is to report back to the class who demonstrated the trait, what the student did, and most important, the effect the student's actions had on another individual. The sequence might sound like this:

TEACHER: Did anyone see someone who was caring today?

JOHN: I did. I saw Jennifer being caring.

TEACHER: What did you see Jennifer do that was caring?

JOHN: I saw her help another student who fell down. She went to the nurse's office to get a Band-Aid and get help.

TEACHER: That was caring. Did you notice how the hurt student felt after Jennifer helped her?

JOHN: Well, at first the student was crying really hard. Jennifer kept talking quietly to her and pretty soon the girl stopped crying.

TEACHER: How do you think the girl felt when Jennifer showed she cared about her?

JOHN: I think she felt better inside.

The dialogue between the teacher and John may have taken no more than a minute, but it was a powerful exchange. The teacher verified not only to John but also to the other students the kind of positive effect caring can have on others. The simple conversation became a significant lesson highlighting the need for learning caring.

STEP 3: SHOW
Teach What the Trait Looks Like and Sounds Like

Now comes the moment when you teach the Character Builder to your students. Very often the prior steps (targeting and defining) are skipped. As a result, many students fail to learn the skills so critical to the trait. There is no perfect way to teach the trait. A few suggested techniques that have been field-tested and proven successful are offered. The most important part of effective teaching is to try and make the trait as "hands on" and meaningful as possible. Never assume students have the language or cognitive acquisition of the trait. Many do not. You can make a significant difference in your students' lives (both now and in the future!) by modeling the trait yourself and making your Character Builder lessons as concrete as possible.

Quick Ways to Show a Character Builder

- Model the trait showing specific behaviors.

- Another staff member can model the trait with you to the class in a quick role play.

- Send a videocamera crew of students on a search for other students modeling the trait. Capture the Character Builder trait on video and then play it for everyone else to see.

- Create, with students, a T-Chart of the skill/trait and, as you develop the chart, model what it looks like and sounds like.

- Identify famous individuals who emulate the skill/trait. Ask students to read biographies about their lives and/or report what the individual specifically did to demonstrate the skill.

- Photograph students demonstrating the trait and make a chart students can refer to.

> "Rudeness is the weak man's imitation of strength."
> —Eric Hoffer

STEP 4: DO

Provide Structured Practice of the Trait

Showing students what the Character Builder looks and sounds like is not enough. In most cases, students must be provided with frequent structured opportunities to practice the new behaviors. In fact, behavior management theory tells us it generally takes 21 days of repetition or practice before a new behavior is acquired. This is an important rule to keep in mind as you try these activities with your students. You will see change if you continue to model the behavior, provide consistent opportunities for students to practice the skill, and reinforce appropriate behaviors. One of the greatest benefits of Character Builders is the program is designed to be used for a minimum of 21 days.

Quick Ways to Practice a Character Builder

- Allow students at least 21 days to practice the skill in frequent structured opportunities.

- Practice sessions can be done in "learning buddies" or "base teams."

- Role play the skill/trait. Younger students can role play Character Builder behaviors using the puppet.

- Students can keep a "reflection log" of their behavior progress with the trait.

- Use any teachable moments to ask: "Is that a stopper or a starter?"

- Character Builder "homework" can be assigned by requiring students to practice the skill at home with their family.

STEP 5: REINFORCE

Give Immediate Feedback and Encourage Use in Life

The final step to teaching a Character Builder is to reinforce students' appropriate behavior or correct inappropriate behavior as soon as it is convenient to do so and encourage them to use the trait in their own lives. There are two important reasons to reinforce the Character Builder trait or skill:

1. It helps clarify to the student that he/she is on the right track and that he/she should keep up the good work. The student immediately recognizes the demonstrated trait because you pointed it out on the spot. Behavior management theory says the student is more likely to repeat the behavior again because he knows what he did right.

2. The reinforced student serves as a model to any other students who happened to be nearby the moment the student was recognized. Keep in mind most social skills are learned through watching others. The frustrating part of teaching for many educators has been the simple fact that appropriate role models are breaking down for our students. Anytime we can use a peer as an appropriate role model and specifically let other students know what the student did that was correct, we are helping those students learn the appropriate behavior.

Quick Ways to Reinforce a Character Builder

- Give specific feedback ASAP: students did the trait right or wrong.

- Tell students exactly what they did right or wrong. If they were correct, say what they did right. If the behavior was wrong, say what they can do next time. Waiting until the end of the day is too late. With some kids, waiting five minutes later is too late. Students benefit from immediate correction.

- Redo the behavior with students on the spot by pointing out or showing exactly what the students should do to replace the incorrect behavior pattern.

- Give students "constructive criticism." Tell what was wrong. Tell what to do to make it right. Be brief. Be private. Be specific and remember: emphasize only the student's behavior, never their character.

- Reinforce to students whenever the skill is done correctly. Use "catching the skill done correctly" as a teachable moment for the rest of the class.

- Provide students with reinforcement tickets, coupons and awards. Character Builders includes a number of these forms for each character trait and skill.

- The Character Builder puppet for each trait can be constantly used as a reinforcer for children. Look for a child who has correctly demonstrated the Character Builder and quietly place the puppet on his/her desk. This child then looks for another student demonstrating the trait and places the puppet on this person's desk. It's a silent reinforcer that tunes students into looking for appropriate behaviors.

STUDENT CHARACTER BUILDERS

One can acquire everything in solitude—except character.
—HENRI BEYLE

Students can be instrumental in helping peers (and staff) "catch a character attitude" by involving them in the planning and implementation of the Character Builder activities. Ideally, these students should be of various ages. This committee can become a core group of students for the year or can be changed monthly. If the committee is to be a school-wide group of students, one or two faculty members can become committee advisors whose job is to coordinate the student group. Possibilities for involving students are endless. Here are a few ideas other school sites have used:

- **Student Campaign Committee.** As each new Character Builder is introduced, the Student Campaign Committee begins a blitz of creating banners, signs and posters to hang up around the school convincing the rest of the students of the merit of the trait.

- **Student Announcement Group.** Many classrooms, as well as schools, begin the day with a one-minute message "advertising" the trait. The advertisement may include a powerful quotation to think about, an announcement reinforcing students "caught" demonstrating the Character Builder or even a quick commercial stating the value of learning the trait. Teachers ask different students daily or weekly to assume this role. Administrators have students make announcements over the school PA system.

- **Skit Committee.** This group of students creates a skit or role play about the Character Builder and performs it at either a school-wide assembly or in each classroom. The skit shows other students the value of the trait as well as what the Character Builder looks and sounds like. (Idea from Lakeview School, Minneapolis.)

> "Human beings can alter their lives by altering their attitudes."
>
> —William James

- **Video Crew.** If you have access to video equipment, you might consider teaching a core group of students how to use it. A student video crew could record actual students demonstrating the trait. They might also video the students' Character Builder skit. The video is then shown in each classroom.

HOW TO USE CHARACTER BUILDER PUPPETS

Developmental learning theory clearly tells us that young children learn best through concrete experiences. The Character Builder puppets in this series were designed with this concept in mind. Each book is accompanied by a puppet as well as stories, role playing and follow-up activities that present the core skills in a meaningful and fun way.

Meet the Character Builder Puppets	
Responsibility Able **Behavior Traits:** He's a star you can always count on; he's dependable, trustworthy, reliable.	**Caring** Sunshine **Behavior Traits::** She's a sun who brings warmth and happness to those she touches.
Respect Admiral **Behavior Traits:** He's a moon you can look up to and admire; he's earned respect through caring actions.	**Disrespect/Negativity** Stinger **Behavior Traits:** He's an unhappy star who puts others down.
Cooperation Pal & Goldie **Behavior Traits:** They are planets who depend on each other; they work together to accomplish their goals.	**Irresponsible** Spinner **Behavior Traits:** He's a comet who has poor judgment and a quick temper; he spins out of control.
Peaceableness Sparky **Behavior Traits:** He's a star who is always positive; he sparkles and shines with builder-uppers.	**Aggressive** Burner **Behavior Traits:** He's a meteor who is belligerent and attacking; he burns himself out.

Note: Larger versions of the above characters can be found in the Puppets section.

The Character Builder puppets will appear periodically in each book to reinforce a trait or skill. If they are to be used in the activity, they will be listed in the materials section. Just look for the gray tone and a small replica of the puppet. A story for younger children using the puppet to describe the Character Builder concepts is then provided.

There are many ways the puppet can be used to liven up the session and reinforce the Character Builder concepts. Here are a few ways the puppet images can be used to make the traits concrete and memorable for young children:

- *Felt Puppet.* To make the puppet durable for years of use, trace and cut the puppet head shape provided in each manual onto felt. Glue the felt shape onto heavy cardboard and cut it out again for a stiff figure. Three dimensional features can be attached to the figure with a glue gun: buttons, movable eyes, yarn hair, pom-poms, and even sequins or rickrack. Finally, attach a wooden dowel to the back of the puppet with heavy masking tape or a glue gun to create a puppet ready to tell character building stories.

- *Paper Stick Puppet.* The easiest way to make any of the Character Builder puppets is simply to duplicate the puppet head provided in the manual onto colored construction paper or cardstock-weight paper. Cut out the shape and tape it to a paper towel tube, a ruler, or a wooden dowel. Students love making their own puppets with you.

- *Paper Bag Puppet.* Duplicate the puppet head onto colored construction paper or cardstock-weight paper, cut out the shape and glue it to the front flap of a lunch-size paper bag. Features can be added to the face or body using items such as colored paper scraps, noodles, egg carton pieces, pipe cleaners, wall paper samples, yarn, bric-a-brac, and fabric.

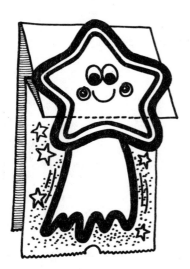

- *Shape Book Cover.* Duplicate the puppet shape onto light-colored construction paper or cardstock. Cut two copies along the outside margin of the shape for a front and back book cover along with several pieces of writing paper so that the cover and writing paper are the same size. Place the writing pages inside the front and back cover and staple the pages along the top or sides. The book may now be used by students to write, draw, dictate further adventure stories about the characters, or describe what they learned in the lesson.

- *Award.* Duplicate the puppet head on cardstock or light-colored construction paper and cut out the shape. Punch two holes along the top, string a long 36" piece of yarn through the holes and tie the ends into a knot. The shape can be hung from the neck of any student who demonstrates the Character Builder trait or behavior.

"I complained
because I had
no shoes until I
met a man
who had no
feet."

—Arabic Proverb

- *Hats.* Fun hats for students to wear while role playing the stories are easy to make. Here are two quick versions:

  1. Fold up the opening on a medium-size grocery bag about two inches. Duplicate a copy of the shape on colored construction paper or cardstock, cut it out and glue or staple it to the front. The student puts the bag on his head for a hat.

  2. Duplicate a copy of the puppet shape on colored construction paper or cardstock and cut it out. Cut a strip of tagboard or construction paper 3" × 28", bring the ends together so they overlap about two inches and staple them. Finally staple the puppet head shape to the front of the strip to wear as a hat.

- *Puppet Bag.* Copy the puppet head shape onto paper and cut it out along the outside edge. Glue or staple the head to the front of a lunch-size brown bag. The opened bag sits on top of students' desks. Use the puppet bags to send notes of encouragement (from you and the students) or to congratulate one another on demonstrating the character trait symbolized by the puppet.

- *Starter and Stopper Puppets.* To help students reflect on appropriate and inappropriate language and behaviors for each of the Character Builder traits, two traffic shapes are included for role playing and storytelling. The Go Sign (page PM15a) signifies "starter" language and behaviors, or the kinds of things people who demonstrate the character trait would say and do. The Stop Sign (page PM15b) represents "stopper" language and behaviors or inappropriate words and actions that do not depict the character trait. The stopper sign is duplicated on red construction paper or cardstock and cut out; the starter sign on green. The signs can easily be made into puppets by gluing, taping or stapling a paper towel tube, ruler or wooden dowel to the back of the shape. The stick is now ready for role playing. The shapes can also be glued to charts, pinned to bulletin boards or taped on a blackboard to enhance a lesson using the skill.

- *Looks Like/Sounds Like Puppets.* To help students recognize the kinds of things people who demonstrate the character trait say and do, two shapes—an ear and an eye—are included in the manual. The ear and eye shapes are duplicated on construction paper and cut out. The shapes can then be glued, taped or stapled to a paper towel tube, ruler or wooden dowel for a stick puppet to use in role playing. The shapes can also be glued to charts, pinned to bulletin boards or taped on a blackboard to enhance a lesson using the concept.

The concrete activities provided in this manual as well as the other four supporting books in this series offer endless possibilities for building the essential character traits in your students. Remember, to help students learn these new skills for now, as well as for the rest of their lives, keep the five steps to enhancing Character Builder skills in mind:

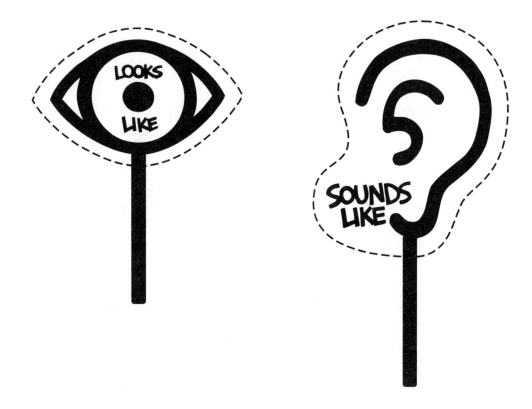

1. **TARGET:** Focus on the Character Builder for at least 21 days.

2. **DEFINE:** Describe the need, value and meaning of the trait.

3. **SHOW:** Teach what the trait looks like and sounds like.

4. **DO:** Provide structured practice of the trait for 21 days.

5. **REINFORCE:** Give immediate feedback and encourage use in life.

 **2**

Increasing Positive Comments and Peaceful Deeds

OBJECTIVES

- Targeting Positive Attitudes and Peacemaking

- Modeling Appropriate Behaviors

- Accentuating the Positive

- Labeling Appropriate Behaviors

- Teaching Character Builder Language and Deeds

- Providing Structured Practice

2

Increasing Positive Comments and Peaceful Deeds

Half the battle is gained if you never allow yourself to say anything gloomy.

—LYDIA M. CHILD

A **"positive climate"**—it's a term you hear quite often in educational jargon these days. Research in school reform verifies that creating a positive learning environment is an essential aspect of creating an "effective school" and preventing dropouts. A positive climate is also essential to peacemaking and character building.

The first building block needed to enhance self-esteem is **security.** A secure learning environment is a place in which children feel emotionally and physically safe. Such a feeling can only exist in an environment that is positive and supportive, that is, one in which students immediately perceive they are welcomed and appreciated. The best way I can find to describe such a place is the opening lines in the title song to the television show *Cheers:* "It's a place where everybody knows your name and everyone's glad you came."

Building a peaceful and positive learning atmosphere is no easy task, particularly when we deal with a negative student, but it is an environment that can be created! Positive language and peaceful behaviors are learned through modeling, conditioning, and/or reinforcement...all elements an educator has control over in a learning setting. Positive attitudes and peacemaking skills, therefore, can be taught. There are six steps to helping students demonstrate more peaceful behaviors and to building a more positive environment. These are:

Steps to Teaching Peaceful Behaviors

1. Target Positive Attitudes and Peacemaking

2. Model Appropriate Behaviors

3. Accentuate the Positive

4. Label Appropriate Behaviors

5. Teach Character Building Language and Deeds

6. Provide Structured Practice

1. Target Positive Attitudes and Peacemaking.

The first step to increasing the character builders of positive attitudes and peacemaking is to target the enhancement of these traits with your students. Changing any kind of behavior involves the following three C's: commitment, consistency, and caring. Begin by deciding to deliberately focus on positive attitudes and peacemaking as new behaviors to teach your students. Then set a goal to focus on enhancing these character builders daily, for a minimum of one month.

2. Model Appropriate Behaviors.

A critical point to keep in mind is that we learn social skills by modeling others who do them correctly. Ask yourself these two questions:

If my students do not have appropriate role models in their lives to model peacemaking and positive behaviors, how will they ever acquire these skills?

How often am I modeling peacemaking and positive behaviors with my students and colleagues?

Never forget the impact you have on your students, and don't downplay the influence you have on them as a role model. According to a study done by the National Parent-Teacher Organization, parents are giving their children eighteen criticisms for every one praise, a ratio of 18 to 1. For many of your students, you may very well be the only appropriate model for peaceful and positive behaviors. Tune in to how often you display appropriate character building behavior and then purposely increase the number of positive messages you send to students.

3. Accentuate the Positive.

To quickly test whether you are "accentuating the positive" in your learning environment, answer this question: *Suppose a visitor comes to your school site for the first time. He or she randomly pulls a student aside and asks him or her one question: "What does your teacher believe in?"" Would the student identify "positive attitudes" and "peacemaking" as important parts of your site?*

If you want your students to be positive peacemakers, it is important that you share your philosophy with them. Tell them how adamantly you feel about not talking negatively about yourself and others. Show them with your own behavior how strongly you believe in this principle. Post signs that emphasize accentuating the positive in highly visible locations, such as on the door, along the length of the chalkboard, or on a bulletin board. As the song goes: "You have to accentuate the positive to eliminate the negative."

4. Label Appropriate Behaviors.

Never make the assumption that students understand what positive and peaceful behaviors look and sound like. Many students benefit from someone specifically pointing out their classmates' appropriate peacemaking actions. It is very helpful to use concrete terms to name positive and negative behaviors. In this program, "Sparkle" is the term used to depict positive language, and "Stinger" is the term used to label negative, inappropriate put-downs. Teach the terms to the students and then consistently use them to label appropriate positive language and peacemaking behaviors as they are performed. For example, when you see or hear a student displaying positive and peacemaking behaviors, take a moment to label them for the students. Always point out specifically what the student did that was positive.

> "Alex, that's a Sparkle because you smiled at your partner."
> "Sharon, that's a Sparkle because you helped Zach pick up his crayons."
> "Kelly, you just gave a Sparkle to Mark because you asked him to play with you."

Specifically labeling students' positive language and peacemaking behaviors is helpful not only to the child who demonstrated the behavior but also to other students who now hear or see an appropriate behavior to model. Negative behaviors can also be specifically pointed out to student but should be done on an individual basis.

> "Jim, that was a Stinger because you told Jason you didn't want to play with him."

5. Teach Positive Language and Peacemaking Deeds.

Some students do not know what positive statements and peacemaking actions are, and so they need to be taught the skills. *Positive Attitudes and Peacemaking for Primary Children* uses stories, posters, and structured role playing as concrete methods to teach the concept of positive attitudes. As a group, you may wish to compile a list of sparkle words, phrases, and deeds on a large sheet of paper as a follow-up activity to each lesson.

Photographs and drawings of positive and peacemaking actions and statements could be included for younger students. A poster with Sparkle Statements has also been included in the program to hang up on a classroom wall. Keep all of these lists visual and continually add to the poster. Students may refer to these posters. Children should be encouraged to refer to the lists frequently.

6. Provide Structured Practice.

A list of Sparkle Statements on a poster, while helpful, is not enough to change students' behaviors. Students must be provided with structured opportunities to practice the new behaviors. The activities in *Positive Attitudes and Peacemaking for Primary Children* are designed for this purpose. An important rule to keep in mind as you try the activity cards is that it generally takes 21 days before a new behavior is acquired. This simply means you won't see improvement by the end of the activity, but you will see change if you continue to model the behavior, provide consistent opportunities for students to practice the skills, and reinforce appropriate behaviors.

WHAT ARE SPARKLES?   PM 1

Purpose: To introduce students to the concept of positive comments and peaceful deeds (or "Sparkles"); to help students recognize the impact their words and actions have to brighten or dim others; to introduce Sparky (a lovable, nice guy character who always says Sparkles to others) and Stinger (The bad guy who says negative comments to others).

Materials: Sparky (PM 1) and Stinger (PM 2) Puppets.

Procedure: *To create the hand puppet:* Cut out two identical puppet shapes from the original pattern. Ideally, you want to cut the shapes out of heavy, non-fraying fabric such as felt. Hand or machine stitch the two shapes together 1/4" from the edges, leaving at least 6" open at the bottom for a hand to fit through. The material can also be attached using a glue gun.

A less durable hand puppet can be made from two pieces of heavy paper, though it will be difficult to bend the shape when the puppet is acting in the scenes. When using material other than felt, cut the puppet at least 1/2" larger than the original pattern. Turn the two pieces right sides facing together and then machine or hand stitch 1/4" from the outside edge.

Now turn the two sewn pieces cut from material or heavy paper inside out. The puppet is now ready to be decorated with movable eyes, yarn hair, a yarn or felt mouth, or any other features of your choice.

To present the story: Prior to delivery of the story, the teacher reads and practices presenting each story using the hand puppet. Feel free to improvise and tell the story in your own words. It is suggested that the teacher begin telling the first story, then switch to Sparky as the spokesperson once the puppet has been introduced to the children. Words in italics are Sparky's; non-italicized words are intended for teachers or students.

Sparky Saves the Planet of Doom

Once upon a time there were two stars who lived in very different parts of the galaxy. Stinger lived on the Planet of Doom. And Sparky lived in Glad Planet Village, a place where everyone got along and seemed to sparkle with happiness.

The Planet of Doom used to be like Glad Planet Village, a happy place where people got along. But everything began to change when Stinger said a put-down to somebody. He was jealous of another star that had a brighter shine than his, so he told the star, "You are the ugliest little star I have ever seen!" The baby star Stinger spoke to felt so bad that he started to cry and the tears started to pour out. The tears started and they wouldn't stop. The baby star cried and cried until the tears put out all of the fire in his star. The light of the little star went out and there was nothing but darkness left where once there was a great brightness.

The Supreme Master of all the Glad Planets was very upset that Stinger had spoken so harshly to the little star. Every star in the galaxy became upset when they heard that Stinger had only just begun putting down other stars. Some of the stars cried themselves away, leaving black holes where there used to be smiles. Other stars decided to join Stinger. Stinger would put down other stars and then these stars would go around putting down still other stars. They would say things to one another like, "You sure are dumb!" or "I don't want to be around you!" Pretty soon everybody on the Planet of Doom became mean and selfish. They made Stan their leader, the leader of the meanies, and named him, appropriately enough, Stinger.

One special star in the galaxy, named Sparky, realized what was going on. (Note: Introduce the Sparky Puppet to the group.) *"On a visit to the Planet of Doom I saw a star frowning and losing its brilliance. Instead of shining and glowing red and yellow, it began to glow black and blue. I was upset. I knew that in a short time the star would burst from unhappiness and all its energy and brilliance would die.*

"That's when I decided I had to do something to bring back the brilliance of the star. I began by teaching this dying star how to say nice things to the other stars like, 'Wow! Outstanding. Awesome. Yes! Great. Thanks!' I called these Sparkle Statements. I noticed that anytime someone said a Sparkle to someone else the star would glow brighter...and brighter. Even dead stars would regain their brilliance and begin to shine again. I came up with a plan. I would go throughout the entire galaxy and ask all the stars to join me. Together we would return to the Planet of Doom and say Sparkles. Perhaps there was still time to save the planet and bring back the stars' brightness.

"I knew lots of stars would be needed to help out since there were far more Stingers on the Planet of Doom than there were Sparkles. The Sparkles would need to outnumber the Stingers if all the stars would shine as brightly as they had before. As fast as I could, I streaked from one constellation to the next asking other stars to join me in an effort to save the Planet of Doom from its terrible fate. Everywhere I went the stars responded, 'We are so glad you came! Yes, we want to stop this darkness before it spreads any further. We will help you make the Planet of Doom shine again.'"

"Soon thousands of stars were ready to travel with me to the Planet of Doom. Together we formed a ring around the first star we came to. At the same exact moment we all joined points and flooded the planet with Sparkle Statements, such as, 'Fantastic! You're special! You're super! I like you. Have a great day!' The next thing we knew, and to our amazement, the black and blue dimness of the star began to fade and the whole planet became brighter and more energized. We then set out to go to every star on the planet and do the same thing to each one." Sparky now asks the audience for help. *"What kinds of words can we say to the other stars to bring back their sparkles?"* Sparky waits to hear the students' responses. *"And that's exactly what we did and said. Soon the whole planet was sparkling again. All of the stars were saved, all that is except Stinger. Stinger refused to listen to any thing any one said, and so he was carried away into the darkness, to live alone in a black hole."*

That's the story of how Sparky saved the Planet of Doom and renamed it the Planet of Delight.

And Sparky learned an important lesson about how our words can make others bright or dim. He learned that *"Stingers are words that make people feel sad and make them black and blue on the inside. I also learned that Sparkles can undo the hurt caused by Stingers. Sparkles are words that make people feel bright and shiny on the inside."*

Sparky says, *"I've come here today to share Sparkles with all of you so you, too, can glow as bright as stars."* (Puppet leaves copy of Sparkle Poster with students.) Sparky continues, *"This poster will help you remember to say words that make your friends sparkle. My star friends are in classrooms all around the world. I'm going to stay here to teach you that you have power in this world. You can make your friends shine just like I helped the stars on the Planet of Doom to shine."*

SPARKLE WORDS

Purpose: To enhance students' awareness of the kinds of positive words they can say to each other. (Before students can say positive statements to others they must be taught what positive statements are.)

Materials: On a 45" square piece of yellow butcher paper, draw a large outline of a "Sparkle" like the one in the drawing below. Outline the shape using a black marking pen and cut it out. Write the caption, "Sparkles," across the top of the shape. You may wish to glue a bit of glitter along the outline of the Sparkle shape.

Procedure: Hang the Sparkle outline on a wall or door. Sparky begins by reminding students of Sparkles and Stingers, as described in the previous session. Sparky asks students to give examples of Sparkle Statements students can say to one another in the classroom or school that would put a smile on someone's face. Using a black marking pen, Sparky writes some positive words inside the outline. These words might include: "Hello! I like you. Thank you! You're nice. Right on. Great. Super! Awesome." Tell students that you want to continue adding words to Sparkles so "we can all be reminded of the kinds of things we can say to others to make them Sparkle inside and out." Explain that the large Sparkle will be left on the wall. As Sparkle Pals, the students' job is to continue listening to others' positive comments so they can find new Sparkles to add to the list. Set aside a brief time each day to read the current list of Sparkles aloud and to ask for new words to print on the shape.

Note: A poster of positive statements entitled "Sparkle Statements" has been included within this manual in the Poster Section (PM 3). You may wish to attach the poster to your classroom wall for students to refer to.

Extension Activities: Write the Sparkle Statements on slips of paper. Place the slips of paper inside a small can or basket placed next to the Sparky Puppet. Whenever a student does a good job or a kind deed, allow that student to take a Sparkle Statement from the pocket. Sparky then reads it to the class and gives the student well-deserved and specific praise for his or her accomplishment.

Sparkle Comments: Print a few Sparkle Statements on large pieces of tagboard. Students love sprinkling glitter on them to make them into real Sparkle Comments. Hang these around the room to remind students to say positive comments to one another.

Literature Suggestions: Here are a few great books which clearly address the themes of peacemaking and positive attitudes. Reading them will help enhance students' awareness that their actions and words have a great impact on the actions and words of others. Consider having Sparky introduce the books to the students and then remain "close by" as the story is read aloud.

The Little Brute Family by Russell Hoban (Dell, 1992). A little family of "Brutes" change their behavior one day when little Brute catches a happy feeling and brings it home. The positive feeling is "caught" by the other family members until they finally recognize their last name of "Brute" is no longer appropriate…thus they become the "nice family." This book appeals to all ages. The moral is powerful, and younger children in particular identify with the characters.

The Quarreling Book by Charlotte Zolotow (Harper & Row, 1963). Here is a little gem. Daddy leaves for work one day and forgets to kiss Mom good-bye. In a short while, the whole family catches negative feelings, until the puppy (with love and licks) helps everyone "re-catch" the positive. Wonderful reading for young children.

The Whipping Boy by Sid Fleischman (Troll, 1986). Here's a Newbery winner, the story of Prince Brat (aptly named) and Jemmy the Orphan together in a tale which teaches children about the power of kindness and how it will eventually win out. The book is suitable as a read-aloud for second-grade students and higher.

The First Forest by John Gile (Worzolla, 1989). In fable form, the author reminds us that greed and selfishness are harmful and that peace and harmony flow from an attitude of grateful appreciation for the gifts we receive and a respect for the need and right of others to share in those gifts.

Slugs by David Greenburg (Little Brown, 1983). This book is definitely humorous and children love it, but make sure you familiarize yourself with it first because to some it's offensive. In lyrical form, it sends the message loud and clear: "Don't expect to be treated any differently than how you treat others."

Somebody Loves You, Mr. Hatch by Eileen Spinelli (Bradbury Press, 1991). An anonymous Valentine changes the life of the unsociable Mr. Hatch, turning him into a laughing friend who helps and appreciates all his neighbors. The book offers a powerful message, clearly showing how kind deeds can impact others in a positive way.

SPARKLE STATEMENTS — PM 3

Purpose: To increase students' awareness of the positive statements they can say to each other.

Materials: Sparkle Statements (PM 3); marking pens; long length of butcher paper.

Procedure: Copy Sparkle Statements and make them accessible to each student; the form could be the basis of an ongoing Sparkle Statement bulletin board.

To construct, cover a bulletin board, door or carrel with butcher paper and copy statements from the form onto the paper. Introduce the board by telling students that statements we say to one another are powerful: they either build us up or tear us down. Tell them that those that build others up are called "sparkles," "builder-uppers," "compliments," or "fuzzies" (choose a term that is appropriate for your students). When students hear positive statements, you or they add them to the list on the butcher paper. To liven up the visual display, Sparky the Puppet form can be duplicated onto several bright-colored pieces of construction paper. Cut out the shapes, sprinkle glitter atop glue in a few places, and hang them up on the bulletin board.

SPARKY SMILE BOOK   PM 4

Purpose: To increase students' awareness of the importance of smiles and to observe smiles in others.

Materials: Making a Smile Book (PM 4); one per student. As students complete each task, which is checked off by the teacher/aide, they may color the numbered space on the sheet corresponding to the task finished.

Procedure: Begin by pointing out what a great smile Sparky has. Sparky explains, *"I smile because I always think positive, happy thoughts about myself and others."* Ask students, "Who else has a great smile?" and invite their responses.

Smile Book: To prepare each book, place five sheets of writing paper on top of a 12 x 9" piece of colored construction paper. Fold the pages in half length-wise and staple along the creases. Number the pages front and back. Students will use the book to write in their responses to each task.

Task 1. Provide students with glue, scissors and an assortment of magazines. Students look through the magazines and find people who smile in ways that appeal to them. They cut out the smiles and glue them to the cover of their Sparky Smile Book. Using a thin-tipped black marking pen, students may write the words "Smile Book" and their name on the cover. They may also use the first blank page as a title page.

Task 2. Each student brings a photograph from home that shows off his/her great smile. They can also draw a self-portrait. Or, you can use a Polaroid camera to photograph their smiles in the classroom. Students glue their photograph or self-portrait on page 2. On the following page, they write about things that make them smile.

Task 3. This task requires a measuring tape and pencil. Students each choose three friends to measure. You may want to pull names from a box to make sure that everyone will be chosen. Students measure the length and width of their classmates' smiles. They write their findings on pages 4 and 5 of the Smile Book.

Task 4. For this task students will need a newspaper, pencil and paste. They read through the newspaper to find a story that makes them smile, then cut it out and paste it on page 6. On page 7, they write why the story makes them smile.

Task 5. Students each find four people on the school grounds whose smiles they admire. They choose from these four categories: adult male, adult female, student male, and student female. Students write their choices and why they picked these people on page 8 and 9 of the Smile Book.

SECRET SPARKY HELLO PERSON   PM 5

Purpose: To increase positive attitudes in the classroom.

Materials:
- Sparky (PM 1).
- Construction paper, glue, hole punch, yarn, pen.

Procedure: To make the badge: Duplicate a copy of Sparky (PM 1) on yellow or orange construction paper. Cut out the shape and either laminate it or glue it to a piece of thin construction paper for durability. Hole punch two holes 1/2" from the top of the pattern. Now lace a 24" length of yarn or string through the two holes and secure the ends with a knot. The Secret Sparky Hello Person can wear the badge. You might print a few Sparkle Statements with a black thin-tipped marking pen (i.e. "Hello," "Hi, how are you?," "It's good seeing you," "Have a great day.").

Begin the activity by assigning one student to be the Secret Sparky Hello Person for the day. The appointed student has two tasks: 1) to keep his/her appointment a secret from the other students, and 2) to count the number of times classmates verbally extend friendly statements toward him/her. Statements that qualify include: "Hi," "Hello," "How do you do?," "How are you?," "Glad to see you," "You look great," etc.

The teacher then tells the class that there is a Secret Sparky Hello Person in their midst whose job it is to keep his/her identify secret and to count the number of times he/she is told the code word/phrase for the day. Tell the class what the code word/phrase is. Note: Consider using simple, non-threatening terms to begin with so that all students are comfortable participating. If verbalizing positive statements is difficult for them, try starting with non-verbal exchanges, such as: pats on the back, handshakes, smiles, eye contact.

When the fifth classmate says the code word/phrase to the Secret Sparky Hello Person, he/she lets everyone in on the secret. This could be performed in a variety of ways:
- the person calls out the code word/phrase or "Hello!"
- the person writes the above on the chalkboard.
- the person calls out "I'm the one!"

The teacher then gives the Sparky badge to that student to wear for the rest of the day. The fifth person who greeted the student receives the Super Sparkle award.

Assign a new Secret Sparky Hello Person for the following day. Change the code each time to reflect a different positive statement or gesture. The class may enjoy introducing the activity to the classroom next door. Soon the class activity will become a school-wide one.

MY SPARKY SMILE FILE   PM 6

Purpose: To increase positive attitudes and the use of builder-upper statements among students.

Materials: My Sparky Smile File (PM 6); two pages duplicated back-to-back on heavy construction or cardstock-weight paper. Fold along dotted lines where indicated on the worksheets.

Staple the file at the outside edges of "In" and "Out" to make pockets.

Cut 1 x 5" strips out of light-colored construction paper. Each student needs the same number of strips as there are students in the class. Students write the name of each classmate on a different strip and put them in the "In" side of the assembled file.

Procedure: Introduce the activity by having Sparky remind students that one way to change a planet from a Planet of Doom to a Glad Planet Village is by saying kind, positive messages to others. Sparky holds up the Sparky Smile File and explains, *"To help each of you to make sure this classroom is a Glad Planet Classroom, I want each of you to use my Smile File for a week."* Sparky asks students: *"What kinds of things can we say to each other that make someone feel happy on the inside?"* The puppet can review a few positive statements by reading the strips from the file and then explain the directions for using the Smile File.

Begin the activity by having students hold their smile files and randomly choose three strips from the In pocket. They read the names and place them in the Out pocket, keeping the names a secret. Sometime during the day students must tell a builder-upper statement to the friends whose names were pulled. You might bring the Sparky Puppet out for this quick review. Students could tell their positive experiences to the puppet. Be sure Sparky provides lavish praise and applause to deserving positive students.

Since much of positive attitudes is learned through modeling, be sure to have a pack of your own. At the end of the day, ask students if they can guess which classmates pulled their names. Ask questions such as:
- How did you know _____ pulled your name?
- What builder-upper statement did your friend tell you?

• Did you hear a builder-upper statement you like that you'd want to use tomorrow?
The following day, students choose three new names and repeat the process until all names have been drawn from the In pocket.

SPARKY SMILE CANS   PM 7

Purpose: To help students learn to say positive comments to each other.

Materials:
- My Sparky Smile File (PM 6); one per student.
- 3 empty juice cans (same size, cleaned with tops removed).
- Popsicle or tongue depressor sticks; one per each class member, including teacher, and 15 extra.
- Glue, scissors, thin-tipped black and red marking pens.
- Contact or construction paper.
- Class photo; copy and circle a different student in each photo (optional: recommended for non-reading students).

Note: Smile Cans may be made for each class member or used as a class activity, in which case only three cans are needed. You may wish to first introduce the project as a group task and as students become familiarized with the activity, change it so that each student has his/her own can. You might have the Sparky Puppet introduce the activity directions to students.

Smile Cans: Cut a piece of contact or construction paper the height, width and length of the three cans and join them with the paper. Use the thin-tipped marking pen to write the words "In" on one can, "Out" on the second can, and "Sparky Smile Words" on the third.

Name Sticks: Use a thin-tipped black marking pen to print vertically the name of each student on the side of a stick. For non-reading students, you may wish to glue a Xeroxed class photo to the top of each stick. Place all the name sticks in the can marked "In."

Positive Comment Sticks: On the remaining 15 sticks use a marking pen to print a different positive comment. Ask students to generate ideas for the comments. You may do this verbally or have them write down their ideas on the form, "Nice Things to Say." Remind them that the comment should be one they can make to anyone (for example, "I like your brown shoes" would not be a good comment) and it must put a smile on someone's face. All comments should be ones you can say, not do, to someone in the class or school.

Spray paint all the Positive Comment Sticks a pale color, or use a different colored marking pen, to distinguish them from the Name Sticks.

Below are some suggestions for positive comments. Add these sticks to the Sparky Smile Words can.
- It's good to see you.
- I like being with you.
- I like you.
- You're a good friend.
- You've got good ideas.
- Have a great day.
- You're fun to be with.
- I'm glad you're here.
- Let's play together.
- Thanks a lot.

Procedure: Begin by randomly electing a student each day to pull one to three names from the In can. Sometime during the day each classmate should be encouraged to say a comment to the chosen peers. Any student who needs a suggestion for a positive comment should pull one from the Sparky Smile Words can. The pulled names are put in the Out can. When no names remain in the In can, all the sticks are placed back in the In can to begin the process again.

Activity Variations:
1. Students have individual Smile Cans. Each day a student pulls one name from the In can and adds it to the Out can when he/she verbalizes a friendly comment to that person.

2. As students enter the room, they pull a name from the In can, read it and place it in the Out can. That person is their Secret Name Pal for the day, to whom they are responsible for saying a positive comment. This way each day every student will give and receive a positive comment.

3. Using the variations above, students pull a name but write or draw a positive comment back to their friend. Keep a large supply of message slips by the Sparky Smile Can for

students to use during the activity.

4. The Sparky Puppet can ask students at the end of the day, *"Who has had someone say something positive to them today? Who was it and what did they say?"* Following each student's positive disclosure, the rest of the class might send a Sparky Cheer. Holding their hands straight out in front of them, students blink, Sparkle their fingers (by moving them quickly back and forth), and say, "We like Sparkles," to reinforce their peer's positive behaviors.

SPARKLE LINE PM 8

Purpose: To create a permanent, visual reminder of the importance of builder-upper statements.

Materials:

To create a *"clothesline of compliments"*:
- Sparkle Boy and Girl (PM 8b); trace pattern onto heavy paper such as tag.
- Long cord or rug yarn of desired length.
- One clip or clothespin for each participant.
- Thick-tipped black and colored marking pens.
- Crayons, glue, scissors.
- Construction paper scraps, rickrack, and metal hooks for attaching clothesline (optional).
- Sparkle Greeting (PM 8a); duplicate a large supply.

Procedure: Students create a figure according to their likeness by tracing the boy or girl pattern onto heavy paper and cutting it out. They then decorate their figures with paper scraps, rickrack, crayons, etc. The teacher writes the student's name on the figure (preferably with a thin-tipped black marking pen), then glues the completed figures onto the clothespins, which are clipped somewhere along the length of the hanging clothesline.

Activity Variations: The actual compliment activity may be carried out in a number of ways. In each of the suggestions below, the complimenter takes a Sparkle Compliment, fills it out and clips it on the recipient's clothespin figure. (This part of the activity applies to those students who can write.)

1. Each day students choose a Secret Pal by randomly pulling the name of a peer from a box containing all the classmates' names on slips of paper (or you can use the Sparky Smile Cans). The puller is responsible for writing a compliment to that student sometime during the day and clipping it to the appropriate figure on the clothesline.

2. Students may also send a positive message to any peer of their choice—particularly someone who has said or done something kind to them.

3. Another way is to choose a student to be the recipient of the Sparkle Greeting for the day. Each classmate writes a compliment to the chosen person and clips it to his/her clothespin. At the end of the day, the recipient collects all the mesages from the class.

4. Encourage students to write messages on special occasions to a peer (thank you, birthday, get well, we miss you, etc.).

Idea adapted from Chick Moorman and Dee Dishon: Our Classroom: We Can Learn Together *(Englewood Cliffs, NJ: Prentice-Hall, 1983).*

SPARKLE BOOK   PM 9

Purpose: To increase students' positive comments and deeds toward one another.

Materials:
- Sparkle Book Cover (PM 9).
- Scissors and hole-punch.
- 24" yarn lengths.
- Writing paper.

Procedure: As students become more proficient in the language of positive statements, start group activities in which students support each other verbally, such as the Sparkle Book.

Make a copy of the Sparkle Book Cover on a double piece of yellow construction paper. Cut around the shape to form the back and front cover of the book. Cut a piece of writing paper for each student from the same pattern.

Each day, choose one student to be the Sparkle Book recipient of the day.

Classmates draw, write or dictate positive comments to their peer on their writing page. At the end of the day, collect all the pages and staple them between the cover. The booklet may be worn by the proud recipient by punching out the two top holes and then stringing it with a 24" piece of yarn. The Sparky Puppet can proudly present the finished book to the student.

SPARKLE GREETINGS BAGS   PM 10

Purpose: To increase positive statements. To practice receiving positive statements from others.

Materials:
- Lunch-size paper bag; one per student.
- Sparkle Book Cover (PM 9); duplicated so that each student receives one from another classmate.
- Sparkle Greeting (PM 8a); duplicated on construction paper, one per student.
- Glue, scissors, crayons.

Procedure: Students decorate their bags by gluing the Sparkle figure to the front. Tape bags to students' desks or pin up on a bulletin board at their eye level.

Each day choose a student (or several) to receive a Sparkle Greeting from their friends. Classmates write the messages on the Sparkle Greeting and insert them inside the appropriate bag(s). The recipients respond to the messages with a verbal or written thank you.

A MONTH OF POSITIVE ATTITUDES   PM 11

Purpose: To help students keep track of their own positive actions.

Materials: A Month of Positive Attitudes (PM 11); one per student.

Procedure: Instruct students to fill in the corresponding dates for the current month writing with small numbers in the upper right-hand column of the squares. At the end of each class day, ask students to reflect upon what positive things they have done throughout the day for themselves and for others. Students quickly note the deed they are most proud of in the corresponding box. Younger students can keep track by drawing a happy (or sad) face in the box that depicts their actions.

HAPPY HAPPENINGS   PM 12

Purpose: To enhance students' awareness and appreciation of the daily positive occurrences in the classroom.

Materials: Happy Happenings (PM 12); construction or cardstock-weight paper for the cover; stapler.

Procedure: Each week appoint a different student to become class secretary. Every day of the week the secretary records positive happenings that have taken place during class time. These could include positive deeds and sayings or classmates as well as special occasions, occurrences, or accomplishments of students. Staple or bind the pages together to form a class journal.

Variation: Individual students can also record their "happy happenings." Make a copy of the form for each student to complete for himself/herself.

SPARKY MASCOT   PM 13

Purpose: To recognize the positive behaviors of classmates. To enhance students' recognition of the positive behavior of others.

Materials: Sparky Puppet (PM 1).

A Special Thank You to Sparky

After Sparky saved the Planet of Doom, the stars decided to recognize Sparky for his good deed. They wanted to tell Sparky how much they appreciated all he had done for them, so they made him a cake and held a party in his honor. They signed their names on a huge card that said, "Sparky, we love you!" and gave it to their friend. Then they presented him with a gift wrapped in yellow paper and red ribbon. When Sparky tore off the paper and opened the box, he found a very special gift. The stars had given Sparky their planet's newly-adopted mascot: an exact copy of Sparky himself. Sparky smiled and said "thank you" to all the stars. *"This is to show how grateful we are to you for having saved our planet. It will bring you good luck,"* the stars told Sparky. Then one of the stars added, *"Sparky, we want you to stay here with us."* All of the stars became even brighter when they heard this suggestion. Sparky had made so many friends on this planet that he immediately agreed to stay. And so for many years Sparky lived on the Planet of Delight, visiting his friends and sharing Sparkles with every one he saw.

Procedure: Have Sparky tell the students: *"Do you know that one of the things that makes me the happiest is when I see someone do something friendly and positive for someone else? There are many ways you can be positive and make others happy. Can anyone tell me one way?"* Take a few minutes to have Sparky elicit from the students a few positive actions, such as "smiling at others," "telling them you hope they feel better," "helping them pick up their crayons," and "patting others on the back." Now Sparky says, *"I know that you do these kinds of positive behaviors all day long, but many times I don't get to see them. I have an idea of how you can let others in this room know they are appreciated for something nice they did. Anytime someone does something kind and positive for you, let that person know you liked what they did by quietly putting me on his/her desk and then quietly walking away. The only rules I have are:*

1. You may not say anything to the person or to anyone else. It's a quiet pass.

2. You may give Sparky to the person only if the person did something kind and thoughtful to you.

3. Someone else may then remove Sparky from that person's desk and quietly pass it to another positive, friendly person.

Sparky will be passed from person to person all day long. This is a quiet way of letting everyone know that people in this room are being special and kind toward one another."

Note: Students generally become very enthused with this activity. The only rule you may have to add is that Sparky must be able to stay on the friendly person's desk for at least five minutes. What often happens is that the puppet is passed so quickly on to another student that the initial recipient doesn't have enough time to enjoy their "reward."

LOOKS LIKE/SOUNDS LIKE

Purpose: To help students understand what the concept of positive attitudes "looks like," "sounds like," and "feels like." To help students understand the meaning of positive attitudes.

Materials:
- Sparky Puppet (PM 1).
- Eye/Ear/Heart Patterns (PM 14a, PM 14b, PM 14c); one copy duplicated on construction paper and cut out. Attach with tape to the blackboard.
- Positive Attitudes (PM 14d); one copy enlarged poster size, duplicated on bright-colored paper and hung on a wall.
- Chalk and blackboard, or chart paper and felt pens.

Procedure: Write the term "positive" on a chart or on the board and ask for meanings from students. Responses might include, saying nice things, seeing the good in things, looking for the best in someone or something, feeling happy and good about yourself and someone else. Sparky can explain the meaning of positive as: *"Seeing the bright side of things; meeting the world in an upbeat and cheerful manner."*

Ask students what positive attitudes "sound like." Use the Sparky puppet to give examples of positive statements, such as: "I like you," "You're special," and "I like doing positive deeds." Write down students' responses as shown on the T-chart on page 41.

Now ask students what positive attitudes "look like." Have Sparky provide a few examples, such as: "smiling" and "sparkling and shining." Write down students' responses to "looks like" on the right side of the T-chart as shown on page 41.

Finally, have Sparky ask students what positive statements "feel like." Tape the red heart-shaped paper to the front of the puppet. Sparky says: "Every time I'm with someone who is positive, I always end up catching their happy feelings. My smile seems to grow. Sometimes I like to hum and I want to do something nice for someone else. Who can tell me about a time someone did something positive for them. What was it and how did it make you feel? Let's write how positive attitudes make you feel."

Add a third column called "feels like" to the chart. Tape up the heart next to the words "feels like" and add a few student comments to the column.

POSITIVE ATTITUDES

Sounds Like	Looks Like	Feels Like
"Good idea!"	Smile	Happy
"I like that."	Pat on the back	Singing
"Great."	High five	Smiling
"Super."	Nod	Good
"It's going to be okay."	Grin	Content
"Don't worry—be happy."	Wink	
"Calm down—think positive."	"Thumbs up"	
"Terrific job."	Sign for okay	
"Wow."	Hug	
"Way to go."	Handshake	
"Looking good."		
"Excellent."		

GO/STOP POSITIVE LANGUAGE PM 14

Procedure: To help students understand the meaning of the trait, positive attitudes.

Materials:
- Sparky Puppet (PM 1).
- Eye/Ear/Heart Patterns (PM 14a, 14b, 14c); one copy duplicated on construction paper.
- Starters and Stoppers (PM 15a and PM 15b); duplicated on red and green construction paper and cut out.
- Masking tape.
- Chalk and blackboard, or chart paper and felt pens.

Procedure: Begin by creating a T-chart. On the blackboard or large chart paper, write the words "Positive Attitudes." Make a large "T" shape under the word. On the left of the "T" write the term "Sounds Like" and to the right of the "T" write "Doesn't Sound Like." Tape the green Starter Sign above the "Sounds Like" section and the red Stopper Sign above "Doesn't Sound Like." Explain that the green "Sounds Like" column are things that positive people say. The Starter Sign stands for GO language, the kinds of things to remember to say because they will help students succeed. The red "Doesn't Sound Like" side of the column on the right, or Stoppers, is for the kinds of statements people who are not positive would say.

To get students thinking about what Starters and Stoppers sound like, use the puppet to give examples of what Sparky would say. For instance, GO statements might include: *"I like to make other people feel good by saying and doing positive things,"* and *"If we make positive statements, we can save ourselves from the Planet of Doom."* STOP statements might include: *"It's no use. Stinger has taken over,"* and *"I wish I could shine as bright as that other star."*

Review the term "positive attitudes" and ask students to think of times they or someone they were with acted or spoke in a positive manner. You might need to provide a few examples: Sally complimented Monica on her new outfit; Ruben encouraged Bill to try his best to pass the math test; Julie patted her friend Kelly on the back when she saw her new sweater was ripped; Michael congratulated Zach by giving him a big handshake when he scored a homerun; Tim's teammates made him a big banner to wish him good luck at his race.

Ask students to think of statements a positive person might say. Write these ideas under the Starters section. If students have a difficult time generating comments, go back to the examples given above. What might Ruben say when Bill says he can't learn to do math?

After a few examples, move to the right side under the STOP section and ask students to think of statements someone who is not being positive might say. Write these examples on the board.

Leave the chart on the wall so additional comments from students can be added under the GO side as they occur in the classroom. Students will begin to focus on positive actions and statements as the trait is accentuated.

POSITIVE ATTITUDES

GO! (Starters)	STOP! (Stoppers)
Sounds Like	**Doesn't Sound Like**
"Good try."	"Lousy job."
"It's okay—you tried your best."	"Can't you ever do anything right?"
"Don't worry—try again."	"Nothing ever works."
"Maybe next time."	"I can't do anything right."
"I'll try again."	"I'm never going to make it."
"You gave it your all."	"You lost it for us."
"Keep it up!"	"Shut up."
"Great!"	"Dumb!"
"Super!"	"What a jerk."
"Think positively."	"Why bother?"
"You'll never know unless you try."	"This is stupid."

SECRET SPARKY FRIEND

PM 14

Purpose: To increase positive, friendly statements toward others. To enhance students' awareness of appropriate positive language and gestures.

Materials:
- Sparky Puppet (PM 1).
- Secret Sparky Friend Badge (see next page); duplicated on bright-colored construction paper. Each day students do the activity, they make two copies of the Secret Sparky Certificate.

Sparky Teaches Good Deeds

Sparky knew that Sparkle Statements alone were not enough to show his friends how special they were to him. Something more was needed. He was glad he had stayed because his work on the Planet of Delight was not yet finished. When Sparky found out some of the stars were having problems making new friends, he invited them to come to his house for lunch so they could get to know one another better. When his fellow stars won an award or achieved their goals, Sparky shook their hands and gave them a pat on the back. And when any one of his friends became sad, Sparky asked what he could do to help him or her feel better. As Sparky told one of his friends, *"It's not enough to just say good things to other people. We need to back up our words with actions. Doing good deeds will show others that we really mean what we say."* Through his actions, Sparky taught the stars on the Planet of Delight the importance of doing good deeds and made the stars glow even brighter than before.

Procedure: Choose one student to be the Secret Sparky Friend for the day. Explain to the student that he/she has two tasks: 1) to keep his/her job as the Secret Sparky Friend a secret from the other students; and 2) to count the number of times classmates verbally extend the Secret Sparkle Statement of the Day to him/her. (With young children, limit the number to five. Explain that the number of statements is the same as they have fingers and to count them by secretly folding down a finger each time they hear a Sparkle Statement.)

Sparky tells the class, *"Somewhere in this room there is a Secret Sparky Friend. This person's job is to keep his/her identity secret and to count the number of times he/she is told the Secret Sparky Statement of the Day. You never can tell who the Secret Sparky friend might be! Today's Sparkle Statement is…"* The teacher, using Sparky, tells the class what the Sparkle Statement for that day is, then adds, *"The rule of the game is to be friendly with as many people as you can in as short a time as possible."* Note: The teacher or the Sparky Puppet should model how to greet another person with these words. Begin with a simple statement such as "Hello" or "Hi" or "How are you?" so that all students feel comfortable participating. Non-verbal exchanges such as pats on the back, handshakes, smiles, and eye contact are also suggested. Choose only one verbal or non-verbal exchange a day.

Sparky says, *"When the fifth classmate says the Sparkle Statement to the Secret Sparky Friend, he/she lets everyone in on the secret by raising both hands up high and yelling 'hello' until everyone sees the Secret Sparky Friend. I'll then give the Sparky Friend Badge to both the Secret Sparky Friend (for doing such a good job of keeping their role secret) and to the fifth classmate who said 'hello.'"*

Assign a new Secret Sparky Friend the following day. Change the code word or exchange to reflect a different positive statement or gesture, such as, "Hi," "Hello," "Have a nice day," a pat on the back, or a handshake.

Extension Activity: Make copies of the Sparky Friend Badge on bright-colored construction paper for each student. A small school photo of the student can be glued in the center of the badge. If possible, laminate the badge for durability. Glue a one-inch magnetic strip to the back of each badge. Present the finished badge as a magnet for students to put on their refrigerators at home as a reminder of Sparky's lessons.

Sparky Pals   PM 17

Purpose: To acknowledge students' positive words and deeds.

Materials:
- Sparky Pal Award (next page); duplicated on bright-colored paper.
- Sparky (PM 1); duplicated on bright yellow paper.

Book Assembly: To create a Sparky Pal Book, fold a 12 x 18" piece of yellow construction paper in half the long way to form an 18 x 6" shape. Staple a few white pieces of 18 x 6" pages inside the booklet. With a black marking pen, print on the cover, "Sparky Pals." Cut out the Sparky figure and paste it on the front of the book.

Procedure: Sparky tells the students: *"One of the things that makes me the happiest is when I see children doing or saying positive words or deeds. I call these children special Sparky Pals. Can you tell me names of positive words or deeds that a Sparky Pal might do?"* Sparky might suggest to the students several examples, such as, helping others pick up their spilled crayons; telling someone who is sad, "I hope you feel better"; asking someone to play with you if he/she is standing alone; and saying to someone, "Nice job!"

Tell the students that during the day Sparky will be watching and listening for Sparky Pals. Explain that when Sparky "catches" a good word or deed, the puppet will write their names down in their Sparky Pal Book (hold up a book for students to see). At the end of each day, Sparky Pals will receive from Sparky a special Sparky Pal Award to take home.

Note: Throughout the day, write down names of students demonstrating positive behavior inside the Sparky Pal Book along with a quick notation to remind you of the students' specific words or deeds. At the end of the day, have Sparky announce to the class the Sparky Pals for the day and briefly describe what they did to deserve a reward. Sparky then gives each Pal an award to take home.

Sparky Pal Award

Awarded to: _____

Date: _____

Authorized Signature: _____

Congratulations!
We're glad you're part of our school.

Extension Activity: Provide students with their own Sparky Pal Books. Ask students to use the book to keep track of their classmate's positive deeds. Every day for a week students draw or write in their books the positive deeds they see others do.

Sparky Ropes

PM 18

Purpose: To increase students' awareness of positive, caring, and thoughtful deeds.

Materials:
- A 36" strip of leather, ribbon, or length of rug yarn.
- Sparky Puppet (PM 1).

Procedure: Tie the rug yarn to one of Sparky's hands. Sparky introduces the activity to students by saying, *"Today I brought a special rope with me. We're going to use it to measure positive deeds. Each time one of you performs a special positive action, I'll tie a knot in the yarn. Let's see how long it will take until the rope is filled with knots from the bottom to the top of the length of yarn. How long do you think it will take?"* Invite students to guess and write their guesses on a chart to refer to again at the end of the activity.

Sparky says, *"Your job is to help me look for positive actions. Each time you see a positive deed being performed (either by someone else or the student personally performing the deed) I want you to remember it."* At the end of each day, Sparky asks the students, *"Who saw or did a positive deed today?"* Sparky then calls on the student who must say the name of the person and what he/she did that was positive. The student and the puppet then tie a knot in the yarn.

Extension Activity: The activity can be extended into a math lesson by measuring the length of yarn at the end of each session. The yarn lengths can then be noted on a chart and graphed. As a follow-up activity, provide students with a 15" yarn length each to take home and try the same activity with their families.

Literature Suggestions: Choose one of the following books on hugs to read to students. Use the read-aloud selections as a catalyst to a discussion about how Sparkles can be words as well as deeds. Make a list with students of the ways we can show others we care for them with our bodies (i.e., pat on the back, eye contact, handshake, hugs, a kiss).

A Book of Hugs by Dave Ross (Thomas Y. Crowell, 1980). This humorous book describes a variety of hugs that can be given to others, such as people hugs, blanket hugs, and birthday hugs. Following the reading, students invent their own unique hugs and handshakes.

Hug Me by Patti Stern (Harper & Row, 1977). A porcupine wants a friend to hug more than anything else in the world.

Sparkle Grams/Awards   `PM 19`

Purpose: To acknowledge students' positive words and deeds.

Materials: Grams and awards duplicated on bright-colored construction paper: Choose from Super Sparkle (PM 19a), Positive Performers (PM 19b), Positive Performance Award (PM 19c), and Gotcha! Ticket (PM 19d).

Procedure: Duplicate an ample supply of the grams and awards. When students perform peaceful actions or say particularly positive statements to others, reward them with a positive note from you.

Sparky Song   `PM 20`

Purpose: To enhance the awareness of the power of positive attitudes on others.

Materials:
- Sparky Song (PM 20); enlarged poster size.
- Sparky Puppet (PM 1).

Procedure: The Sparky Puppet reinforces the power of a positive attitude on others by saying: *"Have you ever noticed the faces on others when they're around someone who is acting positively and saying kind things to others? Show me how these faces look."* Sparky waits for children to smile and then says: *"That's right—they smile.*

"One of the favorite parts of my day is flying over schools and peeking in windows to look for positive classrooms. Whenever I see one person smile, pretty soon another person catches it and puts a smile on too. I sit and watch and see a warm glow all over the room. It's as though all the stars turned their high beams on at once. It's such a happy place.

"Today I have a song I'd like to teach you. The words are all about how wonderful positive attitudes are, and it's sung to the tune of my favorite song, Twinkle Twinkle Little Star." Practice singing "Twinkle Twinkle Little Star" to refresh students' memory of the tune. Sparky can introduce the song to the class by singing the words on the Sparky Song Poster. Students can sing along with the puppet and then begin each day or Sparky Circle by singing the song to remind them of the importance of positive attitudes.

 3

Deflecting Negative Comments

OBJECTIVES

- Identifying Sparkles and Stingers

- Handling Negative Statements

3

Deflecting Negative Comments

The best way to break a bad habit is to drop it.
Habit, if not resisted, soon becomes necessity.

—D.S. YODER

The habit of negativity can be disastrous to children's character development. Negative children very often have low self-esteem because their behavior frequently turns others away. We know what an important role friends play in the acquisition of self-esteem. Having others affirm and approve of us nurtures positive self-perceptions. Negative children are largely handicapped from acquiring feelings of affiliation and belonging.

The habit of pessimism also breeds the debilitating trait of negative self-talk. Not only are these students receiving poor messages from their peers, but they perpetuate the messages inside their heads. While we may hear their degrading messages every so often, research verifies that internally these children are continually bombarding themselves with put-downs. Negativity is obviously a major obstacle to the development of positive self-esteem and positive attitudes.

There's another reason the habit of put-downs needs to be squelched immediately: derogatory comments are deadly to peacemaking. Research suggests that a major reason conflicts escalate to violence is because they began when one person sent an inflammatory put-down or sarcastic comment to another. Obviously, such comments derail a positive learning environment.

What is needed is an all-out assault on negativity, and there's never a better time than when children are young so that habits are easier to change. This chapter helps students recognize the high costs of negativity to peacemaking and a positive climate, and teaches them simple ways to turn put-downs into positive put-ups. There are four steps to beginning the process of creating a peaceable climate.

How to Defuse the Negative

1. Draw Awareness to Negativity.

2. Label the Negative Behavior.

3. Create a Rule: One Stinger = One Sparkle.

4. Teach Positive Self-Talk.

Negative students are not only frustrating but also detrimental to the goal of creating a positive, character building climate. There are several techniques that can be used when students are negative toward themselves or others. It's important to remember that a large part of the success to any of these techniques is consistency. Once you state the rule to the students, you must follow through every time with the same response.

1. Draw Awareness to Negativity.
When students go against the peacemaking and positive attitudes being built in the classroom, be careful not to respond to their negative disposition with more negativity. Casually mention, "Remember, we only say positive things about ourselves," and be quick to point out the positive statements of others. Some teachers use a private code or signal to communicate this idea to their students. Each time students make negative comments, the teacher says a code word like "Zap!" or uses a signal (such as pointing a finger) to remind the students to be positive.

Often students are not aware of how many negative self-statements they are saying; therefore, you will need to bring them to an awareness of just how many there are. One way to do this is to use a simple tally system. Ask students to designate one column on a sheet of paper for positive statements, and the other for negative ones. Each time students make either a positive or negative comment, they add a stamp or mark to the appropriate side.

Another way to reward students for making positive statements is with tokens, such as marbles, poker chips, peanuts, etc. For every positive statement students make, they get to transfer a token from the left to the right pocket, and vice versa for negative statements. Often just one reminder—which requires removing a token from the right pocket and putting it in the left—will get the message of positive attitudes across.

2. Label the Negative.

Teach students to recognize a put-down by saying a code word or by immediately making a sound back to the sender. The code or sound should be agreed upon by all students beforehand so that everyone will recognize when it is being used. Positive Attitudes and Peacemaking for Primary Children uses the word "Stinger." Students are taught that every time they hear a Stinger comment or see a Stinger behavior, they should point their index finger at the offender and quietly say, "That's a Stinger!"

3. Rule: One Stinger = One Sparkle.

Make it a classroom rule that Stinger statements are not allowed. Add to this rule that any time students say a Stinger, they must then change the Stinger into a Sparkle. In some schools this rule is even more stringent: for every put-down the sender must say three put-ups. Whatever the number, the rule must be consistently enforced.

4. Teach Positive Self-Talk.

To teach students positive self-talk, point out the positive attributes in a negative student and then have him or her verbalize them back to you. The attribute being pointed out, though, must be one that really does deserve recognition. For example, you might say, "Roy, you did such a nice job on your paper today. Your letters are written clearly and they are in the spaces. You should be proud of your work. Tell yourself you did a good job." Roy then quietly verbalizes the positive self-statement aloud.

Always conduct this interaction between you and the student only. An individual with low self-esteem humiliates very quickly, and drawing attention to the person in front of others may only exacerbate his or her behavior problem. Keep in mind that individuals with low self-esteem often deny or disregard positive comments because they don't perceive themselves worthy enough to receive your praise. It's a tragic but true premise. Your specific but private reinforcement can be invaluable to helping children form more positive internal images of themselves.

A variation to asking the student to say the comment aloud is to ask the student to say it in his or her head. A simple reminder could be, "You did such a great job today remembering to say Sparkles to others. Did you remember to tell yourself inside your head that you did a great job? Tell yourself right now."

PM 21

Handling Stingers

Purpose: To teach students how to deflect negative comments, then change the Stinger into a Sparkle. In some schools this rule is even more stringent:for every put-down the sender must say three put-ups. Whatever the number, the rule must be consistently enforced.

Materials:
• Sparky (PM 1) and Stinger Puppet (PM 2).
• Toothpicks.

Sparky Gets Rid of Stingers

Sparky says, *"I would like to be able to tell you that all the stars on the Planet of Delight never said another mean thing to one another after Stinger left. But that isn't what happened. Every once in a while a star would forget how much a Stinger could hurt someone else. Then the star would say something that he would later feel sorry he said. What I found out was that it sometimes takes a while to change someone's negative behavior, but you have to keep at it.*

"There is a way to help a Stinger. It's simple. All you have to do is say, 'That's a Stinger.'" (Have students point with both index fingers and say "That's a Stinger.") *"See how easy that was. You don't have to tattle or lecture. You can help these persons simply by letting them know they're dimming someone else's light. Just put up your pointers and say, 'That's a Stinger.'"* (Sparky takes out a toothpick to represent a Stinger.) *"A Stinger is a word with a sharp point on it. It pricks you on the inside and it hurts. It feels like a poke or a stab, like someone has pricked you with a pin."* (Then the puppet breaks the toothpick in half and tosses it over his shoulder.) *"When you say 'That's a Stinger,' you cause the Stinger to lose its power. It won't be able to hurt you or anyone else ever again."*

Sparky invites participation from the students. *"Can anyone give me some examples of Stingers?"* Examples might include: "You're ugly," "You're stupid," "I don't want to play with you," "Shut up," "I don't like you," "Go away." Sparky chooses one of the Stingers and says, *"Now let's practice putting a stop to a Stinger. First you say a Stinger to me."* Students say a Stinger to Sparky who responds by gesturing with two of the points on his star and saying, "That's a Stinger." *"Now it's your turn. I'm going to say a Stinger and I want you to respond as a group."* Sparky says a Stinger like "Go away" and the students point their fingers and say "That's a Stinger." Repeat this part of the activity until the students learn the new behavior.

Sparky says, *"You can help me make your classroom bright just as I did with the Planet of Delight. Every time we get rid of a Stinger together, we'll make our classroom, our whole school, shine a little brighter. We'll help someone shine brighter on the inside. You may not see their light turn on inside, but you may see their eyes twinkle or their mouth turn upward on the outside."*

Extension Activity: Take a few moments to practice with students defusing negativity by pointing and saying, "That's a Stinger." Remind students that they can be most helpful by only pointing and saying the words, "That's a Stinger." They may not tattle to the teacher or criticize the negative offender.

Sparkles and Stingers PM 22

Purpose: To help increase students' awareness of their own power to defuse negative statements. To teach students a concrete technique to combat put-downs.

Materials:
- A piece of 12 x 18" white construction paper folded in half to form a 12 x 9" shape (per student).
- Sparky Puppet (PM 1).
- Stinger Puppet (PM 2).

Preparation: Write the word "Sparkles" on one side of the construction paper and "Stingers" on the other side. For beginning or non-readers, you may wish to glue a bit of glitter next to the word "Sparkles" and tape a toothpick to the side with the word "Stingers" as symbols for the words.

Stingers Hurt!

Sparky begins by saying, *"You may not know just how powerful you are, but it's true! You see, the kinds of words you say to another person can either build them up inside and make them feel happy and glowing, or tear them down so they are sad and gloomy. Sometimes you may not know just how sad you've made them, but if you could see their insides, you'd see it filled with tears. Have you ever had someone say something that made you sad?"* Take a few minutes to have students tell you examples of times when someone made them sad.

Say, *"There's nothing that makes me sadder than hearing words that are sad. I call sad, tearing-down words 'Stingers.' Tearing-down words make me feel inside the same way I feel when I get stung by a bee or prick my finger on a thorn. They hurt! I need you to help me get rid of Stinger words. We need to help people know when they're saying them! Everyone, put your pointer fingers on your left and right hands straight out in front of you."* Show students how to hold out these fingers. Say, *"These are Stingers. Here's my rule. Whenever you hear someone saying a Stinger, help them remember that it hurts. All you have to do is point your Stinger fingers at them and* **quietly** *say, 'That's a Stinger' to let them know they're stinging someone. "Let's practice! Someone says to you, 'I don't like you.' "* Take a few minutes to have students role play combatting other statements from Stinger such as: "That's a dumb idea!" or "I don't want to play with you!" or "That's an ugly outfit!" Emphasize to students that Stinger comments and deeds are not allowed in the classroom or school. They hurt.

Now have Sparky explain that *"the way to take the pain away is with Sparkle Statements. Sparkles are words that make you glow and sparkle, not only on your face, but also on the inside."* Ask students to volunteer to tell about times when people have said or done things to make them sparkle inside. Sparky ends by reminding the students that Sparkle words and deeds are to be the rule in the classroom and that every time they hear or see Stingers to point them out by saying, "That's a Stinger."

Follow-up Activity: Provide a 12 x 18" piece of construction paper per student. Ask each student to draw a picture of a "Sparkle" time and a "Stinger" time in their lives. Tell the students to draw what was happening to make them feel happy and sad. Save the finished drawings for students to share as a group at a following class gathering.

Literature Suggestions: Ridicule, rejection, and teasing—too often they become the vehicles to make a child's life miserable. The following children's literature selections deal with how to handle put-downs. They are excellent to use as read-alouds to help create a dialogue with students after presenting the activity on the concept of Stingers.

Chrysanthemum by Kevin Kenkes (Greenwillow Books, 1991). Chrysanthemum loves her name, until she starts going to school and the other children make fun of it.

Fat, Fat Rose Marie by Lisa Passen (Henry Holt and Co., 1991). A little girl must stand up to the class bully who keeps picking on her overweight friend.

Molly's Pilgrim by Barbara Cohen (Lothrop, Lee & Shepard, 1983). Asked to make a doll like a pilgrim for the Thanksgiving Day display at school, Molly's Jewish mother dresses the doll as she herself dressed before leaving Russia to seek religious freedom. Molly is now ridiculed unmercifully by her classmates for her cultural and religious differences.

The Rag Coat by Lauren Milles (Little, Brown & Co., 1991). Minna proudly wears her new coat made of clothing scraps to school. When the other children laugh at her, she tells them the stories behind the scraps. This is a magnificent tale set in the Appalachian region and illustrated in exquisite watercolors.

The Hundred Dresses by Eleanor Estes (Harcourt Brace Jovanovich, 1972). This is a classic! A third grader is unmercifully teased by her classmates because she always wears the same faded blue dress.

But Names Will Never Hurt Me by Bernard Waber (Houghton Mifflin Co., 1976). A young girl is teased by her classmates because of her name…Alice Wunderland.

Sparkle/Stinger Tallies   PM 23

Purpose: To enhance students' awareness of the frequency of positive and negative behaviors within their classroom or school environment.

Materials: (Per student): A pencil or crayon; a sturdy board about 8 x 11" to write on and serve as a clipboard (such as a book, a piece of cardboard, or an actual clipboard); a piece of 8 x 11" paper folded in half the long way. Teacher needs Sparky Puppet.

Procedure: As adults, we may recognize why positive behavior affects others, but do children? Research tells us that an important step toward successfully assisting students in changing their behavior is to help them recognize why the new behavior is needed. This implies that we need to enhance students' awareness as to why it is important to be positive toward others.

Begin by having Sparky tell the students: *"I think many of you know how important it is to me that we speak kindly and positively to one another. How you treat another person can either put a smile or a frown on their face and make them happy or sad inside, feel bright and shiny, or dim and dark on the inside. Each of you is going to be a detective for today and quietly listen to comments other people are saying to one another. See how often other people in this classroom (or school) are saying Sparkles or Stingers."* Provide each student with a "clipboard," a pencil, and a piece of paper. Ask students to fold the paper in half. On one side of the fold, ask them to write "Sparkle" and on the other side to write "Stinger." (*Note:* For very young children, have them draw a "happy face" on one side and a "sad face" on the other.)

Explain that each time they hear or see a Sparkle they are to make a small tally line or mark on the "Sparkle" ("happy face") side of the paper. And whenever they hear or see a Stinger, they are to make a mark on the "Stinger" ("sad face") side. Ask students to continue the tally all during the day. At the end of the day, collect the finished papers and transfer all the tallies onto a large piece of chart paper. Add up the children's tally marks to assess whether they are hearing and seeing more Sparkles or Stingers.

Note: It is strongly suggested that you role play with the students. Sparky and you can pretend to be secret detectives. You then demonstrate how to make tally marks before students begin the task on their own. This activity could easily be adapted to cooperative learning by pairing students and having them do the task as "Partner Detectives." With older students, extend the activity for a week. Ask students to do the same activity at home as they watch an evening sitcom or Saturday morning cartoon.

Extension Activity: An excellent book to read as an extension to this activity is *Elbert's Bad Word* by Audrey Wood (Harcourt Brace Jovanovich, 1988). Here is a delightful tale about a young boy named Elbert who attends an elegant garden party and shocks the group by using a bad word. A helpful wizard teaches Elbert the important lesson that some words are unacceptable to use in front of others and helps him learn some acceptable substitutes to use instead.

Stinger Burial

Purpose: To help students recognize the destructiveness of put-down statements and to put an end to them.

Materials: A shoebox with the word "Stingers" written on top; a scrap of 3 x 7" paper and pencil per student; a shovel or trowel; toothpicks. Teacher needs the Sparky Puppet.

Procedure: Sparky brings a shoebox and says to students: *"Yesterday, we talked about Stinger Statements and how they can make others feel so sad inside. Who can show me what to do whenever you hear a Stinger comment?"* Wait for a student to give the "That's a Stinger" response. *"That's right! You don't need to give the person a lecture about why you shouldn't use Stingers. But you do need to help people remember not to say them. Pointing it out helps the person remember to stop. Today we're going to get rid of Stingers in this room forever. We're going to bury them!"*

Sparky gives each student a piece of paper and a toothpick (to represent a Stinger) and asks them to find a pencil or crayon. *"I want you to think of a time someone said a Stinger to you. Sometimes you might have been so angry that you said a Stinger yourself. Don't tell anybody what it was you said or the Stinger someone sent you. Instead, write it (or draw it) on the paper. Nobody is going to see your Stinger statement, so cover it up with your hand while you're writing it down.*

Provide a few minutes for writing, then ask students to fold their paper in half so no one can see what they've written. Sparky then opens up the box and calls students one by one to slowly and solemnly put their paper and toothpick inside the box. When all the slips and toothpicks have been stored, Sparky tapes up the box and says: *"Now we're going to get rid of these comments once and for all...we're going to go outside and bury them! Once they're in the ground they're gone from this classroom."* The class and Sparky go outside, and students take turns digging a hole with the shovel. The box is then placed in the ground and covered up with dirt. Sparky says, *"They're gone and can never come back. If you hear someone say a Stinger by mistake, remember all you have to do is turn and say, 'That's a Stinger' to them!"*

4

Accepting Compliments

OBJECTIVES

- Teaching Students to Praise Others
- Recording Good Deeds
- Accepting Compliments

4

Accepting Compliments

I can live for two months on a good compliment.
—MARK TWAIN.

Many of today's students lack the awareness of how to even begin to praise someone and, as a result, their behavior is often awkward, silly or even resistant when teachers ask these students to "turn and praise your neighbor." Praising is a skill that is learned and therefore it can be taught! As you begin infusing this concept into your curriculum, keep in mind the following points:

• Expect students' praises of others to be general and non-specific at first. Only gradually will students begin to make comments that are specific and relate to actual experiences.

• No student should ever be expected to say an insincere "plastic Sparkle." Students should only make statements to one another that they feel comfortable and sincere about.

• You may need to provide a list of sample positive statements students can choose to say to one another. Keep such a list of sample compliments visible for students. After awhile the list will not be needed, since students will have practiced a few key positive phrases in a structured praise session that they can keep as part of their individual repertoires. You may have a few students who will need to refer to the list throughout the year. Respect their need and keep the list accessible.

• Point out that for awhile it is acceptable to say non-specific statements such as, "Hello," "How are you?" and "Have a nice day." These are safe praise openers for beginners to use. Later on, however, raise your expectations so that students do say more specific positive statements. One way to get students to be more specific in their praise is to teach them to add "because…" onto their opening line. Examples include, "I like you **because** you listen to me," or "You look nice today **because** you combed your hair."

• An essential component to teaching students how to praise is modeling the concept yourself. Deliberately increase the number of praise statements you are saying to students. You'll notice students will immediately "catch" the concept. Positive attitudes can become infectious!

Accepting Compliments   PM25

Purpose: To enhance students' awareness of the importance of saying "thank you." To practice receiving compliments by saying "thank you." To learn the three components of receiving compliments—using eye contact, smiling, and responding verbally with "thank you."

Materials: Accepting Compliments (PM 25).

Helping People Sparkle Inside

Sparky tells students: *"One of the things that makes me happiest is to hear Sparkles. It's always special to give Sparkles or compliments to people. Those words make you sparkle inside. When someone says, 'You look great!' or 'I like to be with you!' it makes me glow. There's one important rule about Sparkles: When someone gives you a compliment, it's always nice to let the person know you liked what they told you."*

Sparky says, *"I can do something so easy to make the person who gave me a Sparkle feel special. Let's see if your teacher will start. Will you send me a Sparkle?"* (Note: Teacher responds to Sparky with "yes!" and then says, "We're so glad you came to visit our classroom. You always say such happy thoughts to people and make us feel good! Does anybody want to tell me a Sparkle to make me feel good?") Sparky says to students: *"Now watch what I do...*

> *"I look 'em in the eye*
> *That's the first thing I do.*
> *Then I put on a smile*
> *And say...'Thank you!'"*

Practice the jingle with the students a few times. The jingle is printed on a mini-poster on PM 25. You may wish to refer to the poster with the students as you (and Sparky) teach them the verse.

Students can now role play with Sparky the three elements of receiving compliments: 1. eye contact ("look 'em in the eye"); 2. facial gesture ("then I put on a smile"); and 3. verbal response (And say. . ."Thank you!"). (*Note:* In some cultures, eye contact is not encouraged. If this is the case with your students, please adapt the activity by encouraging students to "nod" their heads in response, instead of using eye contact.) The teacher begins by giving Sparky a compliment. Sparky holds up the poster and points to each line as he reads it. Direct one child at a time to send Sparky a Sparkle statement such as, "We like you," "You're nice," "I like how kind you are." After each student's turn, the class quickly states the jingle and watches Sparky respond appropriately to the compliment.

Extension Activity: Ask students to quickly turn to the person next to them and form partners. In pairs, students practice saying the verse, sending a compliment to their partners, and watching their classmates to see if they do all three elements: use eye contact, smile, and say "thank you." Students can be given a copy of the verse so they can practice the rules of receiving compliments at home.

Sparky Hangings

PM26

Purpose: To increase students' positive comments toward others. To allow each student the opportunity of feeling special.

Materials:
- Sparkle shape cut from yellow construction paper (outline of the Sparky figure on PM 1); one per student.
- Circle with a 5" diameter cut from flesh-colored construction paper; one per student.
- Construction paper cut into 4 x 5" lengths; one per student.
- Yarn cut into 6" lengths.
- Hole punch, glue, glitter, scissors, crayons, and marking pens.
- Sparky Puppet (PM 1).

Face Construction: Students create self-portraits by coloring the circle to represent their faces. Provide mirrors so that physical characteristics are accurate. Strips of colored yarn may be glued to the circle for hair. Other facial features may be added with marking pens, crayons, or pieces of construction paper.

Sparkle Assembly: Glue each child's completed face construction to the middle of the sparkle shape. Colored glitter may be glued to the yellow sparkle if desired.

Procedure: To begin the activity, ask students to sit in a circle with a 4 x 5" card on their lap and a writing instrument. Each day randomly choose a different student to be complimented. The other students then write or draw compliments for the special student and share their cards. Sparky leads the circle discussion by calling on students to share. He asks students to begin their compliment with the word "I…" and then to compliment the student by stating how they feel or think. To get them started, students can be provided with sentence stems, such as "I…," "I feel…," "I think…," or "I am…." Continue doing the activity until every student has had a chance to be the "compliment child." Allow each child a few minutes to practice responding to their compliments by saying to others, "Thank you." Sparky reminds students what he taught them: *"Look 'em in the eye, That's the first thing I do, Then I put on a smile, And say…'Thank you.'"* At the end of the activity, hole punch the compliment cards in the middle of the top and bottom, run yarn through the holes, and hang the cards in a row under the face pattern.

Sparky Pal of the Day

Purpose: To affirm each child's importance and to acknowledge as a class his/her special attributes.

Materials: To construct a "Sparky Pal," each student will need a Sparky figure (copied from PM 1); two 4 x 18" strips of yellow or orange construction paper; one 12 x 18" piece of yellow or white construction paper; black marking pen; staple and scissors; glitter and glue (optional). Teacher uses the Sparky Puppet.

Sparky Bag: Names of each student printed on 3 x 7" paper strips; a sandwich-size bag; a Sparky figure glued onto the front of the bag.

Sparky Pal Hat: Each day create for the Sparky Pal of the Day a Sparky Hat. Cut two 4 x 18" strips from yellow or orange construction paper. Copy the Sparky figure from PM 1.

Attach the Sparky figure to the front of the hat using glue or a stapler. Measure the paper strip around the designated student's head so that the strip can be overlapped about three inches and stapled together at the ends. Glitter can be glued to the front of the hat to create a sparkle effect, if desired. Use a large black marking pen to print the words, "Sparky Pal," across the front of the hat.

Procedure: Sparky tells the students, *"Each day a different student will have the chance to be chosen as the special Sparky Pal of the Day. You will receive a proclamation from me and the other students explaining why you are so special. In addition, you will serve as the official Sparky Keeper of the Day, which allows you to hold Sparky while inside the classroom."*

Sparky begins the activity by expressing a desire to get to know all of the students more personally. The puppet now places all the name cards printed with the students' names into the Sparky bag, mixes them up, and randomly pulls one name from the bag. Sparky reads the name of the student and places the Sparky "crown" on the student's head. The student may be escorted to an official "throne" (a large chair placed near the front of the room just for the occasion).

For the next few minutes, Sparky leads the class in writing a proclamation of specialness to the student which describes what is special about the student (i.e. interests, skills, attributes). The chart could begin with the phrase, "(Student's name) is special to us because...." (*Note:* Tape the 12 x 18" construction paper on a wall or easel. Sparky may hold the marking pen and write down on the chart the positive statements as they are dictated by the rest of the students.) Sparky should remind students that only positive Sparkle statements are allowed. At the conclusion of the activity, roll up the scroll, tie it with a ribbon or rubber band, and allow the student to take it home. Continue the activity by daily acknowledging a different student until all students have been selected. A sample chart is shown below:

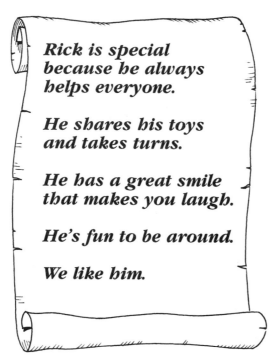

Rick is special because he always helps everyone.

He shares his toys and takes turns.

He has a great smile that makes you laugh.

He's fun to be around.

We like him.

Encourage each student to receive each peer compliment using the three-step method of accepting compliments: 1. use eye contact, 2. smile, and 3. say "thank you."

Literature Suggestions: The following selections focus on helping students recognize their own uniquenesses (the traits, characteristics, talents, and interests that make them special). Following a read-aloud, ask students to think about the question, "What makes you special or unique?" or "What might your classmate tell others about why you're special?"

Just Like Everyone Else by Karla Kuskin (Harper & Row, 1959). A young boy, Jonathan James, appears to be just like everyone else. There is one thing, though, that makes him unique.

I Like Me by Nancy Carlson (Puffin Books, 1988). By admiring her finer points and showing that she can take care of herself and have fun even when there's no one else around, a charming pig proves the best friend you can have is yourself.

Elmer by David McKee (Lothrop, Lee & Shepard, 1968). All the elephants of the jungle are gray, except Elmer, who is a patchwork of brilliant colors. Then one day he gets tired of being different and makes the other elephants laugh.

Quick as a Cricket by Audrey Wood (Child's Play, 1982). A rhymed text and colorful illustrations help create a joyful celebration of self-awareness. This book is a joy.

Tacky the Penguin by Helen Lester (Houghton Mifflin Co., 1988). Tacky the Penguin does not fit in with his sleek and graceful companions, but his odd behavior comes in handy when hunters come with maps and traps.

I Wish I Were a Butterfly by James Howe (Harcourt Brace Jovanovich, 1987). A wise dragonfly helps a despondent cricket realize that he is special in his own way.

The Mixed-Up Chameleon by Eric Carle (Harper & Row, 1984). A bored chameleon wishes it could be more like all the other animals it sees, but soon decides it would rather just be itself.

Sparky Word Gifts

Purpose: To build awareness in students of the power of kind words. To increase students' repertoire of kind words.

Materials: A small, flat box slightly larger than 3 x 5"; wrapping paper, ribbon; large supply of 3 x 5" cards; clear tape, scissors, marking pen.

Box Construction: Wrap the top of the box only with colorful wrapping paper and bow. Make sure the top can still be removed. To the bow attach a greeting card with these words: "Kind words are special presents for a friend." Glue a picture of Sparky on the box.

Procedure: Ask students to tell you words or phrases to say that will put a smile on someone else's face. List these words or phrases on separate index cards. Place the cards inside the Sparky Word Gift box.

Tell students that any time they need to give a Sparky Word Gift to a friend, they may use the cards for ideas. As you catch students saying "word gifts" to one another, encourage them to add their words to the box.

Variation: Make an individual Word Gift box for a birthday student. Classmates all contribute a Word Gift message on an index card and place it in the box for the student to take home on his/her birthday.

Sparky Pals

PM29

Purpose: To provide opportunities to practice friendship-making.

Materials:
- Container such as a basket, hat or bag.
- Students' names printed on strips of paper.
- Sparky Puppet.

Procedure: Begin by having Sparky share examples of friendly words he gives to his friends, such as: *"You're great," "I like the way you shine"*; and deeds, such as pulling out stars that have fallen into black holes, complimenting his friends until they glow, sending them Sparkle Messages reminding them how important their jobs are to the universe. Sparky tells students he does these deeds even though no one else but his friends, and sometimes not even his friends, may know what he did. He says, *"You too have the power to make someone feel good, and when you do, that person may want to become your friend for life."*

To begin the activity, each student pulls the name of a peer out of a hat. This person becomes his/her secret Sparky Pal for the day. Some time during the day, students should secretly do a friendly deed or say friendly words to their pal. At the end of the day, ask each partner to comment on the activities of the day. Did they know who their friend was? What deeds were performed?

Recording Sparky Deeds

PM30

Purpose: To increase students' awareness that words and deeds are friendship-makers.

Materials:
- Recording Sparky Deeds (PM 30); one per student.

Procedure: Explain to students that deeds like the ones Sparky performs are a powerful means of making friendships as well as giving builder-uppers.

Provide students with a copy of Recording Sparky Deeds and encourage them to keep track of the friendly deeds they perform for others. They should write or draw the deed as well as the name of the person for whom they performed the Good Sparky Deed on PM 30 inside each square. Ask students also to think who performed good deeds.

Compliment Hanging

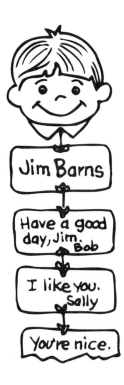

Purpose: To increase students' positive comments to each other and allow each one the opportunity of feeling special.

Materials:
- Compliment Hanging Card (PM 31a); one per student.
- Compliment Hanging Face Pattern (PM 31b); one for the complimented student.
- Yarn cut into 6" lengths; one per student.

Face Construction: Choose a different student each day to be complimented. This student creates a self-portrait by coloring in the Compliment Hanging Face Pattern. Provide a mirror so that physical characteristics are accurate. Then cut out the face pattern.

Procedure: To begin the activity, ask students to sit in a circle with a pre-cut compliment card on their lap and a writing instrument. Each student writes and draws a compliment to the special student and then shares his/her card. Punch compliment cards in the middle of the top and bottom and hang in a continuous length under the face pattern. The cut yarn lengths connect each card. *Note:* The activity can be adapted for non-reading students by having them draw the compliment on the card.

Sparkle Chains

Purpose: To encourage students to recognize the positive actions of others.

Materials:
- One to two boxes of gummed stars.
- 2 x 8" strips of bright-colored construction paper (15 to 20 strips per day, use a different color paper daily).
- Two containers (baskets or shoeboxes).
- Glue or stapler.
- Marking pens and crayons.
- A list of all students' names printed with a black marking pen on a 12 x 36" poster. (The poster can be adapted for non-reading students by attaching a small photograph of each student next to his or her name.)

Procedure: To set up a center for this activity, pin the chart on a wall. Near the chart set up two containers. Fill one container with fifteen to twenty strips of colored paper. The other container is empty and is labeled "Sparky Pals." Provide a supply of crayons and marking pens. Finally, leave the gummed stars in a small box.

Sparky introduces the activity to the students by explaining, *"You have the power to let one another know you appreciate positive deeds and words."* The puppet shows the students the blank strips of construction paper in the container, then says, *"Any time anyone in the classroom has someone do something especially positive or kind toward them, the receiver of the positive deed may thank the sender in a special way. First, print the name of the*

Sparkle Doer on one side of a strip of paper. Then put a gummed star next to the person's name. The star means this person is a special friend of Sparky. On the back of the strip, print your own name and place the strip in the container marked "Sparky Pals." Explain that sometime during the day, you will take the paper strips from the box and Sparky will read the names of the students whose names have a star next to them. The writer of the paper strip will then tell the rest of the class what the student did to deserve the nomination.

Set aside time at the end of each day for Sparky to read the names in the container. As the first name is announced, glue the ends of the paper strip together to form a ring. Pass the next strip through the first ring and glue its ends together to begin a chain. As each new link is added, students will have tangible proof of their positive accomplishments. Sparky reads the compliment to each student as he or she receives it using the three steps of accepting compliments: 1) use eye contact, 2) smile, and 3) say "thank you."

Extension Activity: At the end of each day, the strips may then be graphed to record the number of positive deeds performed on a daily basis.

Literature Suggestions: Below is a list of children's literature dealing with the theme of positive deeds. Each book depicts the theme of caring in a slightly different context and all have a child portraying the role of primary "caregiver."

A Chair for My Mother by Vera B. Williams (Greenwillow, 1982). A child, her waitress mother, and her grandmother save dimes to buy a comfortable armchair after all their furniture is lost in a fire.

A Special Trade by Sally Wittman (Harper & Row, 1978). As a baby, the little girl is pushed in her stroller by her Grandpa. Now she no longer needs the stroller, but Grandpa is in a wheelchair. Thus, the characters make a "special trade."

Maxie by Mildred Kantrowitz (Parents Magazine Press, 1970). An old woman's loneliness is alleviated through the kindness of others in the neighborhood.

Now One Foot, Now the Other by Tomie de Paola (G.P. Putnam's, 1981). A Grandpa once helped his grandchild learn how to walk by citing the refrain, "Now one foot, now the other." When Grandpa has a stroke and must learn how to walk again, it's the grandchild's turn to help.

Stone Fox by John Reynolds Gardiner (Harper & Row, 1980). Willy's grandfather gives up his will to live because he can't raise enough money to pay the back taxes. Willy helps him win the day.

The Cherry Tree by Daisaky Ikeda (Alfred A. Knoph, 1991). After a war destroys their Japanese village and kills their father, the children find hope by nursing a cherry tree through a harsh winter and seeing it blossom into new life.

 The Legend of the Bluebonnet by Tomie DePaola (G.P. Putnam's Sons, 1983). A retelling of the Comanche Indian legend of how a little girl's sacrifice brought the flower called blue bonnet to Texas.

 The Wednesday Surprise by Eve Bunting (Clarion Books, 1989). A young girl helps her illiterate grandmother learn how to read.

 Uncle Willie and the Soup Kitchen by DyAnne DiSalvo Ryan (Morrow Junior Books, 1991). A young boy learns the meaning of giving when he works one day in the soup kitchen.

 Wilfred Gordon McDonald Patridge by Mem Fox (Kane/Miller Books, 1985). A small boy tries to discover the meaning of "memory" so he can help an elderly friend find hers.

The Giving Tree by Shel Silverstein (Harper & Row, 1964). This tender story has become a classic for all ages. The book offers a touching interpretation of the gift of giving and a serene acceptance of another's capacity to love in return.

Sparky Bags **PM33**

Purpose: To increase the use of positive statements. To practice receiving positive statements from others.

Materials:

- Lunch-size paper bags (one per student).
- Decorating materials, such as gummed stars, glitter, marking pens and crayons, and scraps of construction paper.
- Glue and scissors.
- The Sparky figure (PM 1); one per student, duplicated on yellow construction paper.
- An ample supply of light-colored construction paper cut into 3 x 10" strips for stationery.

Procedure:

Provide each student with a lunch-size paper bag. Students decorate their bags with stars, glitter and crayons, then complete it by gluing Sparky to the front. Each student's name is printed on the front of his/her bag using a thick black marking pen. Tape the bags to the students' desks or pin them up on a bulletin board at eye level.

Each day choose a student (or several) to receive a Sparky Greeting from their friends. Classmates draw or write positive messages on the 3 x 10" strips and insert them inside the appropriate bags.

Each day students pull one compliment from their bags. Sparky may assist students in reading their compliment. Each student then walks over to the sender, "looks 'em in the eye, puts a smile on their face, and says 'thank you.'"

Extension Activity: Sparky Bag Puppets can easily be made using the same materials. Glue the Sparky figure on the bottom flap of a lunch-size paper bag. Students can now role play giving and receiving compliments using the Sparky Paper Bag Puppet to help them.

Sparky Book

Purpose: To acknowledge students' positive words and deeds.

Materials: *(Per student)*: Sparky form duplicated on bright-colored construction paper; two 9 x 12" pieces of bright-colored construction paper in a color to contrast with Sparky form; a piece of writing paper; stapler.

Book Assembly: Fold both pieces of 9 x 12" construction paper in half. Cut out the Sparky shape and glue it to the front of the construction paper. Using a thick marking pen, print the words "Sparky Book" across the front cover.

Procedure: Each day choose one student to be the Sparky Book recipient. Classmates draw, write or dictate positive comments about their peer on their writing page. Ask students to begin their comments with the sentence stem, "I like…because…." At the end of the day, collect all the pages and staple them between the covers. Sparky and classmates can then present the book to the child who has been designated as the Sparky Book recipient. The recipient is then encouraged to accept the compliments by using the steps Sparky taught them in PM 25: 1) use eye contact, 2) smile, and 3) say "thank you."

Literature Suggestions: The following read-aloud selections are excellent to use in fostering the concept of giving and accepting compliments:

What I Like by Catherine and Laurence Anholt (G.P. Putnam's Sons, 1991). Rhymed text and illustrations describe a child's likes and dislikes.

I'm Terrific by Marjorie Weinman Sharmat (Scholastic, 1977). A mother bear helps her son, Jason, to recognize just how terrific he really is.

I Like Me! by Nancy Carlson (Puffin Books, 1990). A charming pig describes all the attributes she likes about herself.

I Like to Be Me by Barbara Del Geddes (Viking Press, 1963). This book is a wonderful catalyst to a discussion on, "What is best about you?"

Working in Groups: Sparkle Circles

Circle activities have been specifically designed to include many different grouping possibilities. Sparkle Circles are also a natural way to reinforce the character building skills while enhancing the opportunity to belong. Many of the activities in this section are designed to help children practice giving and receiving compliments. A perfect way to extend any of these tasks is to ask students to sit in a class circle and practice the skill together. This section offers techniques to make the class circle manageable and valuable as a learning tool. I've always found the circle process to be one of the most enjoyable teaching experiences. I had the opportunity to hear my students' ideas as well as share in the development of their learning critical character building skills. The best part is that my students loved them too. Is there any better lesson? The suggested type of grouping for each topic is listed following the circle title:

- **Full.** This means that all students would participate in the circle topic and sit together in one circle. You may wish to consider having cross-age tutors or parent aides participate in the circle as well as facilitate the discussion.

- **Partner.** Some activities are designed so that two students have the opportunity to work with each other on a more interactive basis. Initially, students may wish to work with someone with whom they are familiar and therefore feel more comfortable. After a while, ask students to work with another student they do not know as well.

- **Team.** The team approach is based on cooperative learning concepts. Teams are made up of five to six students representing a broad mix. In one team, for instance, you would place one achiever, one non-achiever, two boys and two girls, one leader and one follower. It is easier to form teams on a permanent basis right from the start so that no time is taken up during the circle activity with planning arrangements.

Some teachers have used the technique of asking students for the names of five students they would like to have on their team. The teacher then forms teams with at least one of the five names on that team. Each team can then design a poster with the names of each member on it. Display the posters during circle time so that students can quickly move into teams.

Teams will need to form an identity for themselves and become comfortable as a group. You may wish to consider doing these activities:

- **Design a Name.** Team members brainstorm a team name, take a vote and then introduce themselves to the larger group.

- **Design a Logo.** Team members brainstorm a team logo and then draw it on a 12 x 18" piece of construction paper. Team members use it as their identity banner.

- **Create a Group Collage.** Provide each team with a large piece of butcher paper, magazines, glue, scissors and pens. Each team designs a group collage on the paper: they glue pictures depicting their individual interests, strengths and desires onto a team collage to represent the whole group. This is then shared with other teams.

Cooperative Learning Tools

The following materials are helpful to facilitate the Sparkle Circle activities. They are merely suggestions and not essential to the activities; however, many teachers have found them useful.

- **Puppets.** The puppet introduces the Sparkle Circle activities and facilitates the discussion. Any puppet that is friendly-looking will be sufficient. The Sparky Puppet provided in this manual can help remind students to say builder-upper statements to each other.

- **Timer.** This can greatly facilitate circle discussions because it lets students know visually and audibly when the circle time is up. A clock timer is best. Set the timer for the designated time (20 minutes or so) and tell students that when the timer buzzes, the circle is over.

- **Suggestion Box.** A shoebox with a removable lid will suffice. Cut a slit 1/2 x 5" along the top of the box. Decorate it with stickers or wrapping paper and write "Suggestions" along the side. Encourage students to place inside the box suggestions for future Sparkle Circle topics.

- **Name Cards.** Make a set of name cards on 3 x 5" strips of cardstock-weight material. Print the names of half your students in red ink; the remaining half in another color ink.

You may also wish to paste a Xeroxed photograph of each student on their respective card.

- **Listening Book.** Make a Listening Book ditto like the illustration that appears here. The sheet should have space for each student's name. Make several copies of the sheet and staple them between construction paper covers. Use the book during circle time to keep a record of students' comments; it is also an incentive for listening.

On selected circles, name the topic at the top of the form and then quickly jot down the main idea of each student's contribution. At the end of the circle, ask students if they can remember facts about their friends (Who was listening!). For example, "Who in this classroom is afraid of the dark?" (Scott) "…of spiders?" (Sally).

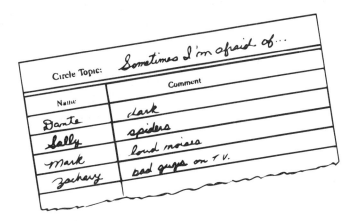

- **Pass-Around-the-Prop.** Several activities suggest a prop featuring the group topic for students to pass around the circle. A prop instantly reminds younger children whose turn it is and how much longer it will be until their turn comes.

Sparkle Circle Rules   PM35

Grouping: Full.

Props: Create a poster using bright-colored construction paper or cardstock. A few suggested rules for concept circles follow. You can describe these rules in your Sparkle Circle to your students or adapt them for your classroom. While in your circle, you might write them on a poster for children to refer to during the circle time.

Paper Circle: Cut out one yellow 12 x 16" construction paper circle. Sprinkle glitter over glue on the circle and allow to dry. Cut out yellow construction paper into 6" circles, one for each student as well as for yourself.

Option: Sprinkle glitter over glue that has been placed around the edge of each circle in the outline of the student's name to make name tags. Divide the circle into four even sections.

Procedure: *Note:* With younger students it is effective to use a puppet each time to introduce the circle topic and review the rules. Explain to students what a Sparkle Circle is, its objective and the rules for the circles. Here is a suggested script to serve as a guide:

"Today is a special day because it is the first time we get to meet in our Sparkle Circle. This is a time when we will gather together, share our ideas and feelings, and listen to the thoughts and feelings of our friends. This is a time when we want to learn new things about each other and build each other up.

"Just like our classroom and school have rules, this circle also has rules. I've written them on this chart to help us remember." (Show the chart.) "The first rule says **Stay seated**. You may choose where you want to sit in the circle. Sometimes I will ask you to sit in a special place. Once you sit down, please stay there; you may not move." This is the time to introduce the Sparky Puppet who "helps us remember the rules." Sparky can sprinkle some pretend glue on the ground each time to help students remember where to sit and not to move.

"The second rule says **Say only Sparkles**. This is the most important rule. In this circle we want to make sure everyone feels included and happy about being here. You can make people feel that way by the kinds of words you say." (Sparky can share a few Sparkle statements, for instance, complimenting some of the students seated in the circle.) "I want you to think for a minute just how powerful you can be as a Sparkle to another person. We want everyone to have good, positive feelings about themselves and that's why we have a rule to say only Sparkles.

"Every time someone says a Stinger to someone it tears away a bit of their good feelings about themselves." (Demonstrate by tearing a piece through the middle of the yellow circle.) "It's hard to mend broken feelings. You may hear other people saying unkind Stinger statements to others. Lots of them. We do know we can change broken feelings by saying lots of Sparkle statements. Stingers are so powerful that, after hearing one of those, a person needs almost ten positive statements to feel better inside. Remember, we only say Sparkle comments to each other. When you talk, please remember to use calm, positive voices so everyone in the circle can hear you.

"The third rule is **Listen to the comments of others—don't interrupt.** You will have a chance to speak, so please make sure you allow everyone to have their full turn. You can make the speaker feel more comfortable by looking at him or her and smiling or nodding to show you are really listening." (Demonstrate these behaviors using the Sparky Puppet. Thank Sparky for listening.)

"The fourth rule is to **Take turns**. Everyone will have a chance to speak in this circle and everyone's ideas count. All our ideas are equal—just like the circle we're sitting in. You'll know it's your turn because we will be passing around a friendly reminder.

"You may also want to plan your comment. Each time we have a Sparkle Circle, I will give you a few minutes to think what you'd like to say about the circle topic. Do it then so when it's your turn, you'll know exactly what to say. It will make the circles go much faster.

"One more thing to remember is that **It's OK to pass**. We want to hear everyone's ideas, but sometimes you may not want to talk about that topic. You have that option, and all you have to say is 'Pass' (Sparky says, *'I pass.'*). "Hopefully, you won't choose to do it too often because then we won't have a chance to find out about you." You may wish to inform students how often and how long each circle will meet. You can then introduce the timer that is set for the number of minutes you have planned for the circle.

Pass a yellow circle (called "Sparkles") to each student. Ask students to write their name on the tag in large letters. (These can be pre-printed for non-writing students.) Students turn to the person on their right and exchange name tags. These partners are now a team. Tell them that they have three minutes each in which to find out their partner's name and favorite hobby or interest. The interviewer draws a picture in one section of the partner's circle and signs his/her name. The partner now does the same. At the end of six minutes, teams rejoin the circle. Each partner now "introduces" the teammate by stating his/her name and interest. (Encourage reticent students to show the drawing they have made.)

Use the Sparky Puppet to ask students to name one thing they learned about a classmate that they didn't know before. Close the circle by thanking students for their participation.

Sparkle Circle   PM36

Purpose: To help students practice verbalizing positive statements toward their classmates.

Materials: Sparky Puppet.

Procedure: Ask the students to sit on the floor in a tight circle. Sparky asks the students, *"What kinds of Sparkle Statements could you say to someone in this class to make them feel happy?"* Sparky can elicit ideas from the students and suggest other statements. Sparkle comments could include, "I like you," "You're nice," "I like playing with you," "I'm glad I know you," and "Have a nice day." Comments could be written on a chart or blackboard for students to refer to.

Sparky now tells students, *"Today we will be having a Sparkle Circle where we can practice giving Sparkle Statements to one another. Each of you will give one Sparkle Statement to one person, and you in turn will receive one Sparkle Statement from another person. Everyone point to the person in the circle on your right."* (Note: Students may need some help in identifying their right side.) *"That's the person you will be giving a Sparkle Statement to. Take a moment and think what you will say when it is your turn."* (Pause for a few seconds of "think time" for students to think through what they will say.) *"Who remembers what you do when you are given a compliment?"* Sparky calls on one student to respond. The puppet then helps students recall the "thank you" verse learned at an earlier session: *"Yes, I look 'em in the eye, that's the first thing I do. Then I put on a smile and say, 'Thank you!'"* Sparky then tells the students: *"To help you remember whose turn it is to send the Sparkle Statement, I am going to move around the circle. I'm going to start with your teacher and he/she is going to be the first person to send the Sparkle to the person on his/her right side. Just remember to send me gently!"*

The Sparkle Circle activity begins with the teacher modeling the first Sparkle Statement to the person on his/her right. The receiver then says "thank you" and takes Sparky. This student then sends a compliment to the student on his/her right and the activity continues until all students have had a turn.

Self-Praise

One of the characteristics of children with high self-esteem is their ability to praise themselves realistically. This doesn't necessarily mean they are overly boastful and bragging (in fact, such a trait is often a common indicator of low self-esteem). Individuals with high self-esteem recognize their strengths and accept their weaknesses. They don't have to continually remind themselves of their talents—they recognize their attributes with an inner quiet confidence. The value of teaching young children to praise themselves is so they will in turn catch the habit and acknowledge themselves internally—and that, in a nutshell, is the whole secret of self-esteem enhancement.

As educators, our goal is to help young children learn to praise themselves so they can develop the habit of becoming their own reinforcer. Children with the highest self-esteem don't need us to constantly pat them on the back and acknowledge their skills with external rewards. These children are not externally driven—they are self-propelled. The development of internal empowerment is a slow process, but one in which educators can make a noticeable difference.

There's one more value to teaching self-praise. Many researchers have found that once children learn to acknowledge themselves, complimenting and acknowledging others is a much easier development. It is the next step to a more positive and peaceful learning climate.

The following Sparkle Circle activities are designed to help students learn to praise themselves.

How Do You Do?   PM37

Grouping: Full/Team

Procedure: Students sit in the circle. Begin by having the Sparky Puppet introduce himself to the class. *"My name is Sparky and I have five points on my star."* The first student begins by introducing himself/herself and states one thing that would describe a physical attribute:

> *"My name is _____ and I have _____.*
> For example: *"My name is Ryan and I have blue eyes."*

The student immediately on the right speaks next and starts by introducing the person who previously spoke.

> *"This is _____ and he/she has _____.*

The circle continues until each student has introduced the person immediately preceding.

Listen Up!   PM38

Grouping: Full/Team.

Materials: The Sparky Paper Bag Puppet (described on page 78) may be used as a prop.

Procedure: The first student begins the circle by introducing himself/herself and stating one thing he/she enjoys doing. *For example:* "Hi! My name is Zachary, and I like to play baseball."

Continue in this manner around the circle until all students have had the opportunity to introduce themselves. The student who originated the circle then introduces his/her "next-door circle neighbor" by stating the person's name and the interest that was already expressed. *For example:* "This is my friend Brooke, and she likes to dress up."

Continue until all students have introduced the person sitting immediately next to them.

Ball Pass

Grouping: Full

Materials: One medium-sized ball (or beanbag).

Procedure: The first person begins by holding the ball and saying:

> *"My name is _____ and I like to _____."*

The speaker then tosses the ball to another participant who in turn says:

> *"Hi _____"* (repeating the name of the former participant),
> *"my name is _____ and I like to _____."*

The ball continues to be passed around the room until all participants have had the opportunity to catch the ball.

Body Tracings

Grouping: Team.

Materials:
- Large sheet of butcher paper measuring the length of the students; one per student.
- Scissors and marking pens.

Procedure: Divide students into teams of four to five members. Each day one student on the team lies down on the paper and has his/her body outlined by another student. The teammates now have five minutes to ask the student any questions about his/her interests, past, family or competencies. The questioned student has the right to pass on any questions. The questioning period must stop at the end of the set time.

The team now has five minutes to fill in the outline with words, slogans or drawings that represent their findings. Each completed body outline is then "introduced to the class." The team "reads" their findings to all students. This activity will take as many meeting times as the number of team members.

Design a Logo

PM41

Grouping: Team.

Materials: 12 x 18" piece of light-colored construction paper for each team of four students. (They may also do this on an individual basis.)

Procedure: Students design an insignia or logo for Concept Circles. If students are in a support team of four to five members, they will design a logo for just their team. Each team (or individual) shares their logo. These can later be placed on T-shirts, banners or posters to encourage team affiliation.

Me Bag

PM42

Grouping: Full/Team.

Materials: Small lunch bag per student; glue, scissors, magazines.

Procedure: Students write their names at the top of one side of the bag. Tell them to look through the magazines and find slogans, words or pictures that describe themselves. They glue the pictures on one side of the bag only.

You may wish to set the timer for a specified time. When the time is up, everyone takes a turn explaining their bag to other students (or to their Support Team). *Note:* To save class time the bag can be sent home as an evening home assignment and brought back the following day. Save the bags for Me Bags by Others (PM 54) and Me Bag Compliments (PM 55).

								Jerry	Brad	Mary	blue
							Ruth	Harry	Lisa	Bruce	red
										Pat	green
		Zach	Adam	Jill	Bryan	Burt	Fred	Bill	Mort	Mary	yellow

Our Favorite Colors

I Like

PM43

Grouping: Full.

Materials: A shoebox or similar-sized box; cover with wrapping paper/contact paper and glue a mirror on top of the box. Teacher uses Sparky Puppet.

Procedure: Begin by having Sparky sing or say the following rhyme:

Mirror, mirror on the box,
My face in you I see.
There are so many things I like,
Just because I'm me!

Sparky teaches the children how to say the jingle. Then he shares some of the things he likes, such as: smiles, sparkles, the color yellow, and a clear night sky.

Each student says the jingle (with the help of other friends) while holding the box and then states one thing he/she likes. Students enjoy drawing a picture of a favorite thing they like before the circle starts. When it is their turn they can then place the drawing inside the box.

Variations: Change the format so that each time the box is used the I Like item becomes more specific.

"I like the color_____."
"I like the book _____."
"I like to eat _____."
"I like to watch _____." (TV or movie)
"I like to play _____."

You can easily graph each topic for students to see each other's choices (see illustration on page 88). Students paste their drawings next to their choice on a large piece of butcher paper.

I Like to Be Me

PM44

Grouping: Full.

Materials: *I Like to Be Me* by Barbara Bel Geddes (Viking Press, 1963). Read the book to the students, or the Sparky Puppet can tell the story. This is a wonderful motivator. The book lends itself to the flannel board.

Procedure: Sparky begins the activity by saying, *"I'm glad to be me because I shine."* Then the first student in the circle says, "I'm glad to be me because I'm cute." The second student says exactly what the first student stated ("Sally is glad to be Sally because she is cute") and then follows with why he or she likes to be himself/herself ("And I'm glad to be me because I'm a good soccer player"). Continue moving around the circle in this manner. Students can help recall others' positive statements as the list increases.

Note: Write down the students' self-statements exactly as they say them. At a later date print these comments surrounded by self-portraits on a large sheet of butcher paper for a bulletin board.

I'm Great!

PM45

Grouping: Full/Team.

Materials: Large bag of small food items such as candy, raisins, small marshmallows or cereal; container to hold them.

Procedure: On the first day of the circle, pass the container around the circle with the food items inside. Instruct students to take one piece only. Before eating the food, students must say one statement describing themselves. In the beginning these could include statements about interests (favorite food, movie, TV show, etc.) or physical characteristics. With each succeeding circle increase the amount of food items by one (for instance, on the fourth circle, each student would take four pieces from the container, say four self-descriptive comments, and then eat the food).

Note: You may wish to make a chart or words or pictorial representations of the types of descriptive comments students could say. First circles should always be nonthreatening and focus on concrete descriptions. Favorite things are always safe topics. Only gradually will students feel secure enough to describe more abstract thoughts and feelings about themselves.

Variation: Consider using non-food items as rewards, such as trinkets, writing accessories, stickers, etc.

Idea suggested by Leona Leist; New Richmond School District, New Richmond, Ohio.

A Me Hanging   **PM46**

Grouping: Full/Team.

Materials: 5" light-colored construction paper circles—cut four for each student; crayons, hole-punch, yarn lengths, glue, magazines.

Procedure: Provide each student with four circles. On each circle students depict an interest or something they like. They may represent their interests with words, phrases, drawings or magazine cutouts. Instruct students to fold completed circles in half.

Each circle day, students share one completed circle with the rest of their classmates by stating and showing what they like.

Variation: Take a circle, which is folded in half, and glue one half of it back-to-back to half of another circle. Do this to each circle until all four are joined together to form a sphere. Punch a hole in the top of the sphere and thread a yarn length through the hole. Tie it securely and hang the sphere from the ceiling to form Me Hangings.

Praising Others

Circle topics that increase friendship and peacemaking generally follow on those designed to increase students' sense of selfhood. Individuals must feel secure and confident in their identity before they can genuinely compliment others and take pride in their achievements. When students learn to praise themselves, praising others comes almost automatically.

Many students feel uncomfortable praising another student because compliments may not be part of their repertoire. Let them know that if they need help in thinking of a compliment they may choose one from available sources such as the Sparkle Statements (PM 3) or the ideas generated by students in Sparkle Word Gifts (PM 48).

Sparkles in a Circle   **PM47**

Groupings: Full/Team.

Materials:
- A large star (at least 20") cut from yellow or orange tagboard. (Using a black marking pen, draw a "Sparky face" and print the words "Sparkle Statements" inside the circle.)
- A "Sparkle" (a 6" star shape) cut from yellow or orange construction paper; one per student.
- Black crayons or marking pens.

Procedure: Review the Sparkle Circle Rules with students. Emphasize the importance of saying Sparkles because "they make us glow on the inside." Tell them that there will be many opportunities in circles to say Sparkle statements to each other. Not only is it important to say them, but it is also important to accept them. Ask them what they could say if someone gave them a compliment. Three acceptance phrases are:

- Thank you.
- I'm glad you noticed.
- I appreciate that.

Divide students into teams of two (or four). Ask each team to think of statements they could say to someone in this class or school that would put a smile on his/her face. These statements should be general so that anyone could say it to anyone else ("I like your curly hair" would not be general enough).

Pass a Sparkle (construction paper star) to each student and ask them to write or draw a Sparkle comment on each star. Students then rejoin the circle and present the compliment to the student on their left. The receiving student should be encouraged to respond with one of the four accepting comments.

To conclude, display all the Sparkle statements around the edge of the large star. Keep the poster in the room to use with each Sparkle Circle. Students may refer to the list of ways to accept compliments from time to time.

Sparkle Word Gifts   PM48

Grouping: Full/Team.

Materials: 4 x 6" cards; one per student.

Word Gift Box: Cover the top only of a gift box with wrapping paper in such a way that the top of the box can still be lifted.

Procedure: Ask students in the circle to state words, phrases and sentences that would "put a smile on someone's face." Write each comment on a separate 4 x 6" card and place it in the box, which is then passed around the circle. Students take turns choosing a phrase from the box and saying it to their neighbor. Encourage the recipient to accept the comment with an "acceptance phrase."

Periodically add new word gifts to the box as they are stated or suggested by the students. Remind them that "The words we say are gifts we can give to one another." You may wish to write a card on the top of the box that reads: "Kind words are special presents from a friend."

Variation: In future circles use the box to ask students to compliment another student. The box may be kept in the middle of the circle. Any time students wish to validate another student they may use an idea from the gift box.

Sparkle Box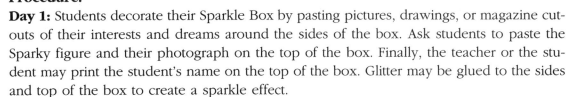

Purpose: To provide students with the opportunity to practice giving as well as receiving compliments.

Materials:

Day 1: *(Per student):* Cut out Sparky figure (on PM 1) and duplicate on bright-colored construction paper; a photograph of each student; a shoebox; glue, scissors, and glitter; magazines or construction paper scraps. Teacher uses the Sparky Puppet.

Day 2: *(For each circle activity, per student):* A 4 x 6" piece of light-colored construction paper and a crayon or pencil.

Procedure:

Day 1: Students decorate their Sparkle Box by pasting pictures, drawings, or magazine cutouts of their interests and dreams around the sides of the box. Ask students to paste the Sparky figure and their photograph on the top of the box. Finally, the teacher or the student may print the student's name on the top of the box. Glitter may be glued to the sides and top of the box to create a sparkle effect.

Day 2: Ask students to bring their Sparkle Boxes with them and to gather together in a Sparkle Circle. Distribute a 4 x 6" paper along with a crayon or pencil to each student. The puppet then describes the activity to students by saying: *"Today we are going to give a Sparkle gift to the person on our right. Will everyone take a moment to find who the person sitting on your right side is?"* (Students may need help locating their right-side friend.) *"Take a moment and think of something you know that's special about that person. Maybe you know they are a good artist or a singer or reader. Maybe you like to be with them because they share or they have a nice smile. And sometimes you may not know the person who is next to you that well. That's all right too. Does anyone know some things you could tell a person you don't know very well?"* Elicit some ideas from the students; the teacher can also pass on some ideas.

Sparky now says, *"Everyone take a moment to think about what you'd like to draw or write to the person on your right. When you're ready, draw the Sparkle idea you'd like to tell them. Don't let them see it…make it be a surprise!"* Allow two minutes for students to draw, then ask them to sign their name to the card. Sparky then quickly reviews the rules of the

Sparkle Circle: *"Each person will have a chance to hand their card to the person on their right and tell them about their Sparkle idea. When you get the card, you may put it inside your Sparkle Box. Remember, whenever someone sends you a Sparkle, you look 'em in the eye, that's the first thing you do, then you put on a smile and say 'thank you!'"* Students take turns moving around the circle handing their card to the student on their right and saying a Sparkle Statement about the student. The student then responds with "thank you!" and places the card inside their Sparkle Box. Continue the activity every day for a week, asking students each day to sit next to a different student.

Sparkle Boxes can remain on the tops of students' desks or on a book shelf throughout the month so students can send special "Sparkle word gifts" to one another. The activity can easily be varied by choosing one student each day to be the recipient of Sparkle card comments from all of their classmates. Choose a different student each day until all students have had the opportunity to become the recipient of the word gifts.

Sparky Stick Puppet

Purpose: To teach students how to send and receive compliments from their peers in a positive manner.

Materials: *(Per student):* Cut out Sparky figure (PM 1) and duplicate on yellow construction paper; one popsicle stick, tongue depressor, or plastic straw; one 3" strip of masking tape.

Puppet Assembly: Students create Sparky Stick Puppets by taping the back of the Sparky figure to a stick.

Procedure: Sparky introduces the activity to students by inviting them to make a puppet just like himself/herself. Sparky asks students to bring their puppets with them and gather together to make a Sparkle Circle. As a quick review, the puppet asks students to tell him/her the second Sparkle Circle rule: *"Only say Sparkle Statements, and when someone sends you a Sparkle Statement, I look 'em in the eye, that's the first thing I do, then I put on a smile and say 'thank you!'"* Sparky tells students: *"Today we're going to learn a new Sparkle rhyme. You say it whenever you hold your Sparky puppet stick.* (Teach students the rhyme on the mini-poster PM 20.) *The rhyme is sung to the tune of "Twinkle Twinkle Little Star" and goes like this:*

> **Sparky, Sparky, we love you.**
> **You help us sparkle. Yes, you do.**
> **Your Sparkles make us shine so bright.**
> **Our classroom now is full of light.**
> **Sparky, Sparky, we love you.**
> **You help us sparkle. Yes, you do.**

Students sit in a circle on the ground and take turns giving compliments (Sparkles) to the person sitting to their right. The Sparkle receiver holds his/her Sparky puppet and recites the jingle. Encourage other students to recite the jingle at the same time. When the student receives the compliment, he/she uses eye contact, smiles, and says "thank you."

Extension Activity: Invite students to take the Sparky Puppet home with them to introduce Sparky to their families and to practice sending Sparky Statements around the dinner table or at some other convenient family gathering. Extra Sparky Puppet samples could be left in a basket in the classroom for students to role play sending and receiving compliments with one another. *Note:* Save the Sparky Stick Puppets to use for a role playing activity in Sending I Messages (PM 67).

Sparkle Banners   PM51

Grouping: Partner/Full.

Materials:
- 12 x 18" construction paper; one per student.
- Scissors, crayons or marking pens.

Procedure: Each student cuts out a banner shape. Students then form a "partnership" with another student they do not know well. Students have three minutes each to interview their partners, with the purpose of finding out about their partner's interests, background, family, unique competencies, etc.

At the end of six minutes, students have five to ten minutes to construct a banner about their partners. The banner should have the partner's name printed in large colorful letters as well as words or pictures representing the student's discoveries. Everyone shares the banners with the entire group.

Riddles   PM52

Grouping: Full/Team.

Materials: Slip of paper 5-1/2 x 8-1/2" for each student.

Procedure: Tell students their task is to write a riddle about themselves on the paper. The riddle should include clues about:
- physical characteristics;
- an interest or hobby;
- where the student is most likely to be found.

Students include their name on the back righthand corner of the card. To save time, the riddle card should be a homework activity. Students who do not read or write need a parent or aide to help them with the task. Younger students can draw the riddles and provide only one clue on a card.

Students place the completed riddles in a container and pass them counterclockwise around the circle. The first student pulls a card from the container and reads it (or has it read to him/her). He/she then tries to guess who the student may be. If the person guesses correctly, he/she may present the card to the student. If the student chooses incorrectly, however, any two other students may try to guess.

The activity continues around the circle until all the cards are distributed. The game may stop at any time and be continued as time permits. Students who are last to guess will obviously have the advantage. Point out that it is because they had to wait longer.

Silent Sparkles   PM53

Grouping: Full/Team.

Procedure: Begin by asking students to think of ways they could put smiles on other people's faces *without saying anything* (mention that these are called actions). List the suggestions on a large piece of chart paper. You may wish to keep the chart in a permanent place so that you can add additional ideas. Actions may include:

• hugs
• holding hands
• handshakes
• pats
• smiles
• looking at the person (eye contact)
• listening to the person
• sharing something
• sitting by someone
• spending time with the person
• walking up to someone.

Learn the song "Hugs" (or change the words to any of the above-mentioned friendly actions). You can sing it to the tune of "Mary Had a Little Lamb."

> *A hug is something if you give it away,*
> *Give it away, give it away...*
> *A hug is something if you give it away,*
> *You end up having more!*

It's just like a magic penny.
Hold it tight and you don't have any.
Lend it, spend it, and you'll have so many,
They'll roll all over the floor.

Repeat chorus changing hug to smile, pat, handshake….

Students perform an appropriate, friendly action toward the student sitting immediately to their right. *Note:* Some students will be very uncomfortable giving and receiving hugs and that should be respected. Smiles and handshakes are fine!

Follow-up Activity: Read to students *A Book of Hugs* by Dave Ross (Thomas Y. Crowell, 1980). Have students draw a picture of a friendly action they might do for someone else. Collect the pages and bind them together as a Class Book of Friendly Actions.

Me Bags by Others   PM54

Grouping: Full/Team.

Materials: Me Bags (saved from PM 42); magazines, scissors, glue.

Procedure: Students sit in support teams. A different team member is the focus for each Sparkle Circle. Other team members cut out magazine pictures, words or slogans that somehow depict the student. These are glued on the remaining side of the bag. Each group then shares the bag with the class explaining what they've learned about that member.

Me Bag Compliments   PM55

Grouping: Full/Team.

Materials: Me Bags (from previous circle); 3 x 5" index cards *(one per student)*.

Procedure: Choose one student to be the recipient of compliments. Give the remaining students each an index card and ask them to write or draw a compliment to the student. Students sit in a circle with the student's Me Bag in the center and take turns saying the compliment before putting it in the bag.

Note: This is a good closing activity. As it takes a short time to do, each session could end with a compliment writing (or drawing) finale, focusing on several students in turn.

5

Using I Messages
to Solve Conflicts

OBJECTIVES

- Increasing Sensitivity to Others' Emotions
- Expressing an Emotion Vocabulary
- Learning Constructive Ways to Deal with Emotions
- Learning the Peacemaking Technique of I Messages

 **5**

Using I Messages
to Solve Conflicts

Educate your children to self-control...and you have done
much to abolish misery from their future lives
and crimes from society.
—DANIEL WEBSTER

Perhaps one of the greatest peacemaking skills we can teach children is how to stop a conflict from ever starting. Far too many problems quickly escalate into aggressive disputes simply because the victims don't know how to stop the ascent. Here is the typical scenario:

Sally and Ryan are at recess playing four square. Ryan is the server and Sally is giving it her all to try and win the serve. What Sally doesn't know is that seconds before getting in line to wait her turn to play, Ryan and the other players have established the rule—a liner is out. Sally's only played the game with a liner called in. Here comes Ryan's serve to Sally and it ends up on the line. Now watch the scene as a simple problem quickly becomes a full-scale battle.

1. Ryan calls the ball out.
2. Sally calls the ball in.
3. Ryan tells Sally to leave.
4. Sally yells back at Ryan, telling him she's staying and calling him "stupid."
5. Ryan's temper mounts and he yells back at Sally calling her "dumb."
6. Sally throws the ball at Ryan, hitting him in the head.
7. Two students on the sidelines decide to "help" out and by the time the teacher gets to the scene four students are in a full-scale fighting match.

Whether it be at the four square court, lunch line, school bus, or classroom, such scenes of escalating violence are all too common. Research on violence clearly tells us the problem could have been prevented or greatly minimized if the students had used a "defuser" skill back at step four. Instead of Sally yelling at Ryan and building his anger, she could have told him her concerns using a technique called an "I Message" developed by Dr. Thomas Gordon. An I Message—or calmly telling the person your feelings, and stating the problem or what you want to happen—is a defuser skill because it reduces the aggression or the potential for violence.

We know one of the greatest causes of aggression is the use of sarcasm, name-calling and put-downs. An I Message is a powerful peacemaking skill for children to learn because it teaches them a simple but effective tool for derailing the conflict. The students instead address the problem because they have learned that put-downs and an uncalm demeanor are sure ways to exacerbate the problem.

This section teaches young children what an I Message is and why it is effective, then provides opportunities to practice the skill. Make sure to provide at least 21 days of practice because an I Message is a Character Builder skill that will help our children become better peacemakers for life.

Identifying Emotions: First Step to I Messages

The importance and pervasiveness of emotions in our lives hardly needs debating. Emotions are fundamental to human nature; they enrich our lives and, when ignored, may cause problems or lack of interest in life. Exploring their emotions helps students better understand themselves and others.

Before sending I Messages, students need to identify what they are feeling. The activities in this section on feelings are designed with the following purposes in mind:

• To increase students' awareness and sensitivity to the fact that not everyone reacts to the same experience in the same manner.

• To help them explore their own emotions and thereby further develop self-understanding.

• Encourage the use of constructive ways to deal with their feelings.

• Assist in conflict situations (a student who verbalizes feelings will be less likely to use physical means to resolve a relationship problem).

• Increase awareness of what is personally valued.

Emotion education is a critical Character Builder because it helps students clarify and sharpen their self-picture and thus develop a stronger sense of selfhood.

Dictionary of Feelings

PM56

Purpose: To help students learn the words that identify emotions and to increase awareness of feelings.

Materials: Dictionary of Feelings (PM 56); colored paper for dictionary cover; crayons or marking pens; paste or glue; stapler and scissors.

Dictionary Construction: Duplicate the Dictionary of Feelings so that you have one copy of each page for every student. The cover page should be a bright color; the interior pages can be white. Photocopy so that pages 1/14 are on the back of the cover; 3/12 on the back of 13/2; 5/10 on the back of 11/4; and 7/8 on the back of 9/6. Collate, fold in half, and staple the book together along the center fold.

Procedure: Introduce the dictionary to the students, perhaps with a discussion of how important emotions are. Students fill out the cover with their name and the copyright date.

On the day that the students write about a specific emotion, discuss it with them and show them pictures that illustrate the feeling. You may also read a story that depicts the subject matter. Students then work on the page that correlates with the emotion discussed.

For each emotion, the following activities may be performed:

1. The class can formulate their own definition. (Consider having real dictionaries on hand as models.) Write class definitions next to the emotion word. A few definitions to incorporate include:
   - angry—mad
   - happy—glad
   - proud—feeling special
   - lonely—being by yourself
   - sad—unhappy
   - scared—afraid
   - silly—having fun

2. Students illustrate the emotion by depicting themselves feeling that emotion.

3. Students write about a time they remember when they felt that way. Younger students dictate their stories.

4. On the facing page, students may paste or glue pictures from magazines that illustrate the emotion.

Feelings Wheel

PM57

Purpose: To increase students' sensitivity to the emotions of others, as well as make them aware of their own emotional fluctuations.

Materials:
- Feelings Wheel (PM 57).
- Light-colored construction paper or cardstock.
- Two-pronged paper fasteners, hole-punch and scissors.

Procedure: Duplicate the top and bottom sections of Feelings Wheel onto heavy paper. Cut out the sections, placing them on top of each other. Connect the wheels with a paper fastener.

Wheels may be kept on students' desks or worn (punch a hole at the top of the bottom wheel section and tie it with a 24" yarn length). Encourage students to identify their changing emotions by moving the dial. Invite classmates to be sensitive to their peer's feelings by observing each other's wheels. Encourage sympathetic words and gestures when a peer's wheel indicates a troubled time.

Sparkle Circle Activities

The next activities continue to help students develop an awareness of feelings and identify emotions, but are conducted in classroom Sparkle Circles. Many teachers find that students profit from expressing their feelings in a group, because it instantly allows skills such as accepting compliments, sending I messages, saying thank you, and using eye contact to be practiced. The more students can practice these skills the greater the likelihood they will master them and call them their own. Any of these activities can easily be adapted to a paired student activity or even an individual task.

Feeling Drawings

PM58

Grouping: Team.

Materials: Record player or tape recorder; 12 x 18" drawing paper, one per student; crayons or marking pens.

Records depicting different emotions:

- *Sadness:*   Anton Dvorak, "Symphony No. 5 in E Minor"
                 Peter Ilich Tschaikovsky, "Symphony No. 6 in B Minor"

- *Anger:* Modest Mussorgsky, "Night on Bare Mountain"
  Paul A. Dukas, "The Sorcerer's Apprentice"
  Claude Debussy, "The Sea (La Mer)"

- *Happiness:* Maurice Ravel, "Bolero"
  Anton Dvorak, "Carnival Overture"
  Peter Ilich Tschaikovsky, "Nutcracker Suite"

- *Fear:* Gustav Holst, "Mercury" from "The Planets"
  Edvard Grieg, "Peer Gynt"

- *Playful:* Camille Saint-Saens, "Carnival of the Animals"

Procedure: For each Sparkle Circle activity, students listen to a different musical selection that depicts an emotion. Using crayons or marking pens, students express their feelings by moving the crayons across the paper. At the conclusion of the activity, students dictate or write their reactions to the musical selection on the bottom or back of the paper by completing the appropriate sentence stem:

- *I feel (angry, sad, happy, scared) when* _____.
- *Something that makes me feel* _____ *is* _____.
- *A time when I felt* _____ *was* _____.
- *When I feel* _____, *I usually like to* _____.

Happy/Sad Beanbag   PM59

Grouping: Full.

Materials: Make a circular beanbag (at least 8" in diameter) from plain-colored fabric. Stuff it with beans or rice. Use felt scraps and glue to make a happy face on the front and a sad face on the back.

Procedure: Toss the bag to each student in the circle. Students verbalize back to you and the group a situation that causes them to feel the emotion shown face up on the bag. They then toss the bag back to you for a new toss.

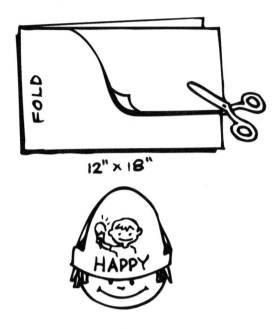

Emotion Hats

PM60

Grouping: Full.

Materials: *Emotion Hat (one per student):* Cut the hat from a strip of construction paper (12 x 18") and staple the ends at the back. On the front, print the emotion term to be discussed that day.

Procedure: Following a discussion about a particular emotion, students draw a picture on the front of their hat to represent a situation that causes them to feel that way. They then wear their hats during circle time when they share their feelings.

Feelings Thermometer

PM61

Grouping: Full.

Materials: *Thermometer Construction:* Make a large thermometer from a heavy piece of paper at least 12 x 20". Draw faces (or use cutouts) vertically along the thermometer depicting each of the following emotions: happiness, sadness, fear, anger, pride, etc.

Punch a hole in the middle of the board 2" from the top and 2" from the bottom. Thread large rug yarn (red and white, 9" of each tied together) between the two holes.

Procedure: Pass the thermometer from student to student in the circle and ask them to put the red yarn next to the face that represents how they feel that day. (They pull the yarn until the red comes up to the place they want.)

Variation: Set the red yarn to a certain emotion and pass the thermometer from student to student while asking them to comment on when they felt that way.

Student Thermometers

Grouping: Full.

Materials: Paper plates (for thermometers); glue, magazine pictures, scissors; paper fasteners; black construction paper scraps.

Procedure: Students make their own thermometers. They find magazine pictures that depict the different emotions they are studying and glue them around the edge of a paper plate. Cut an arrow from black construction paper and fasten it to the center of the plate with a brad. Students turn their arrow to the emotion that best represents their answer to sentence stems such as those below:

- When I'm in a dark room I feel…
- On the first day of school I feel…

- On my birthday, I feel…
- During reading I feel…
- Talking in front of the class makes me feel…
- When I come to school each morning, I feel…
- When it's time for circles, I feel…
- Friends make me feel…
- The people in this classroom make me feel…
- During music time I feel…
- When I get my papers back, I feel…
- During spelling tests I feel…
- When someone tells me they like me I feel…
- When my best friend is sick, I feel…
- When someone smiles at me, I feel…
- At recess time I feel…

Feeling Masks   PM63

Grouping: Full.

Materials: Feeling Masks (one per student): Cut from 9 x 12" tagboard-weight paper into circles.

Mask Construction: Put on facial features and staple or glue each mask to a ruler, pencil or skewer. The faces illustrated here or those on Feelings Thermometer (PM 61) can serve as patterns.

Procedure: The masks can be used for various purposes in the Sparkle Circles.

- *Role Play:* In turn, students choose one of the masks, place it in front of their faces, and act out a time when they felt that way.

- *Individual Mask:* Use a different mask for each circle. In turn, students place the mask in front of them and describe a time when they felt that way.

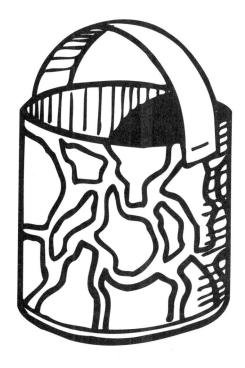

Wishing Well

Grouping: Full.

Materials: Brown and gray construction paper; ice cream carton (available from ice cream stores).

Wishing Well Construction: Glue torn pieces of brown and gray construction paper onto a large ice cream carton, tearing paper freely into "stone shapes." Staple a paper handle across the top.

Coins: Cut 6" construction paper circles for each student.

Procedure: Instruct students to draw a self-portrait on one side of the coin and on the flip side draw a picture of something they would like to wish for. Students in turn toss their coin into the well, which is placed in the middle of the circle, and say the rhyme:

> *I wish upon the coin I drew.*
> *I'll toss it in for hopes come true.*

Variation: Read a book to the students on the theme of wishing:
Alexander and the Wind-up Mouse by Leo Lionni (Pantheon, 1969).
Sylvester and the Magic Pebble by William Steig (Simon & Schuster, 1969).
The Little Rabbit Who Wanted Red Wings by Carolyn Sherwin Bailey (Platt and Munk, 1978).

Accepting Differences

Young children are by nature egocentric and must first see the world from their own point of view. As soon as you notice students can identify and name different emotions, it's time to help them decipher the feelings of others. The following activities help children practice identifying the emotions they learned in previous activities but now they are asked to determine the emotions of their peers. This is the first critical step towards empathy and accepting differences in others.

I Feel...You Feel   PM65

Purpose: To help students develop a deeper understanding of the importance of accepting differences in others.

Materials:
• I Feel/You Feel (PM 65); enlarged to poster size.
• Two 5" round circles cut from construction paper (per student).
• Sparky Puppet.

Face Construction: The students color a happy face on one of the circles and a sad face on the other. Then they paste the circles back to back on the end of a popsicle stick, tongue depressor or straw. Make one extra stick face for Sparky to hold during the lesson.

Procedure: (*Note:* Young children often think and feel as though the world revolves around them, so it can be difficult for them to see someone else's view. Repeated experiences listening to the views of others is a helpful way to develop empathy for others.) Sparky asks students to form a large circle. The puppet says, *"Everyone has different feelings. Sometimes I like things that the other stars don't like, and sometimes they like things that I don't like. But that doesn't mean we can't all get along and make our place a Planet of Delight. All of you have different views and opinions. You like different things and you do things in different ways. And it's ok. That's what makes the world an interesting place to live in."*

Sparky distributes the happy/sad sticks to the students. Sparky also has a stick. He now reads a few of the issues below and asks the children to share their feelings by turning their sticks either to the happy face or to the sad face. Sparky reminds the children there are no right or wrong answers. (*Note:* Begin with a nonthreatening question such as, "How do you feel about pumpkin pie?") Sparky turns his stick to the sad face and finds a student with a different view. The puppet then sings the following jingle while showing the I Feel/You Feel poster to the class:

> ***I feel happy and you feel sad (or I feel sad and you feel happy).***
> ***I guess everyone has a different view.***
> ***That's what makes me...me, and you...you!***

Sparky may wish to briefly ask the student to explain why he or she chose the feeling he or she did regarding the issue. The puppet quickly teaches the students the jingle and continues raising other issues, such as:

- How do you feel when the teacher calls on you?
- How do you feel about broccoli?
- How do you feel about playing jump rope?
- How do you feel about reading?
- How do you feel when it rains all day?
- How do you feel in the dark?
- How do you feel when it's time for school?
- How do you feel when it's your turn to share?

Sparky leads the activity and says the jingle until a few children catch on to the jingle. You may want to write the words on the blackboard or on chart paper for children to follow along as you sing. Allow them to fill in the jingle with the words "happy" or "sad":

_____ (name) feels _____ and _____ (name) feels _____ .
I guess everyone has a different view.
That's what makes me...me, and you...you!

Literature Suggestions: The following selections are wonderful catalysts to any discussion regarding "a different point of view." Read the book aloud to students and ask them to use the formula above with the two different characters.

The Pain and the Great One by Judy Blume (Dell, 1984). This picture book is written from two perspectives and in two parts. The older sister ("The Great One") thinks her younger brother is a bothersome pain who gets too much parental attention. The younger brother ("The Pain"), from his perspective, thinks his sister gets too much love just because she's older.

The True Story of the Three Little Pigs by Jon Scieszka (Viking, 1989). The wolf gives his own outlandish version of what really happened when he tangled with the three little pigs.

The Bedspread by Sylvia Fair (William Morrow, 1982). Two elderly sisters embroider the home of their childhood at both ends of a white bedspread. Each depicts the home as she remembers it with surprising results. The book's message is that everyone has a different viewpoint and there may be no one correct view.

Bea and Mr. Jones by Amy Schwartz (Puffin, 1983). Tired of kindergarten, Bea Jones trades "jobs" with her father who works in an office.

Encounter by Jane Yolen (Harcourt Brace Jovanovich, 1992). A Taino Indian boy on the island of San Salvador recounts the landing of Columbus and his men in 1492. While most stories about the first encounter are from Columbus' point of view, Yolen thought it would be interesting for the readers to hear a Taino boy speak.

Through Grandpa's Eyes by Patricia MacLachlan (Harper & Row, 1980). A young boy learns a different way of seeing the world from his blind grandfather.

Solving Problems Peacefully

`PM66`

Purpose: To help students learn to cope with the emotions of anger and frustration appropriately. To provide opportunities for students to use appropriate emotional language to defuse conflict.

Materials: Sparky Puppet (PM 1) and Staying Calm Poster (PM 74).

Sparky: The Problem Solver

Sparky says, *"For the first time in many years, everyone on the Planet of Delight was happy and getting along with one another. They knew how to say Sparkles to make each other shine. They knew how to stop Stingers. They also knew how to do good deeds and how to accept compliments. There was only one more thing to be done: I decided to visit Stinger in his black hole to see if there was any way I could turn him around. Boy, was I in for a rough ride!*

"I thought I was ready for any of the Stingers that might come my way, but what he did took me completely by surprise. He stole my magic wand (Sparky waves wand). *Without my wand, I could no longer travel instantly from one planet to another. I would be stuck here in this black hole with Stinger for the rest of my life. He hadn't even bothered to say hello before he grabbed it out of my hand, then he began waving it in the air and said he would break my wand in half if I came any closer.*

"I didn't know what to do. If I started to cry, my sparkles would dim and my fur would become all tangled. If I didn't do or say anything, the Stinger would win. He would keep my magic wand and he would be free to go and come as he pleased and I would be stuck here. At that moment, I was so angry I felt like a volcano that was ready to explode. I wanted to punch and kick Stinger or say a bad Stinger back to him, but that would only have made him into a volcano too. I needed to calm down, so I slowly started counting to 10. This would give me a chance to think what to do. One, two, three, four.... So, what can I do? Can you help me with this problem?" (Sparky listens and responds to children's suggestions.) Display the poster, staying calm, to students.

"Well, here's what I did. I didn't call Stinger names and I didn't hit him. I just told him how I felt. I told him I felt angry and I told him why I felt angry—because he took my magic wand. And then I told him what I wanted him to do. **'I feel angry because you took my wand and I want you to give it back to me.'** *The first time I said it he laughed and tried to ignore me. Then I looked him straight in the eye and said it again,* **'I'm angry that you took my wand and I want you to give it back to me—now!'** *He saw the anger in my eyes and heard the certainty in my voice. He knew I was serious. He got so scared he backed himself up into a corner and this time he did what I asked, he gave me back my wand. He never tried that trick with me again. That I Message helped me avoid getting into a big fight with Stinger."*

Sparky sums up what he learned from this experience. *"I used something called an I Message. An I Message is a way to tell someone you are upset without getting them upset too. It's a good way to solve a problem with someone who does or says something to make you sad or angry, frustrated or scared, embarrassed or unhappy. It might be that someone has pulled your hair, or punched your nose, or poked fun at the way you look. If you don't do anything, this person will just keep on doing whatever he or she is doing. And if you pull, punch or poke back, the two of you will end up in a fight and someone could get hurt. An I Message lets you stand up for yourself without making the problem worse. You'll be able to solve your own problems the way I did with Stinger. After giving me back my wand, Stinger said he felt really bad about all the trouble he caused me and the other stars. We left the black hole together and returned to the Planet of Delight where the other stars taught him how to live with them in peace."*

Sending I Messages   PM67

Purpose: To teach students the technique of I Messages as a method of dealing with conflicts. To help students learn to cope with the emotions of anger and frustration.

Materials: I Messages (PM 67); enlarged to poster size. Hang in the classroom as a visual reference for students. Students can be given copies of the poster to take home so they can explain the concept to their parents.

Procedure: I Messages represent a powerful technique to teach students how to deal with conflict. All children at one time or another encounter times of frustration and difficulty. There are appropriate and inappropriate ways for them to deal with their frustration and anger. How they verbalize their frustrations may make all the difference as to whether the situation is escalated or minimized. I Messages are a way for students to tell another person they are upset without insulting, blaming, or calling names. Teachers who have taken the time to teach the concept say that students are frequently able to solve their own conflicts without adult assistance. The number of classroom conflicts are minimized because students have a tool to use in preventing full-scale conflicts from materializing.

It is important to keep in mind that children need continued practice with this method before it will become automatic. Any time an actual problem comes up in class, use the problem as an opportunity for students to apply I Messages to the situation. Add role playing to the situations described in this section to supplement the examples. And, finally, teachers should never forget how powerful they are in their role as Character Builders in the classroom. Any time I Messages can be used with the students, do so!

Note: For very young students, teach only the first and second parts of the I Message: "I feel…when you…." Eliminate the last part of the formula, "and I want you to…," in order to simplify the activity. It's always a nice addition to any comment to say "please" at the end. Tell students that "please" is a magical word that Sparky loves because it always makes any place of doom turn into a glad place.

Sparky introduces the activity by saying: *"I wish people would use Sparkle comments all the time. Everywhere would be such a happy place to be. Unfortunately, though, I hear a lot of Stinger Statements. They always make me feel so sad and sometimes they even make me feel angry inside. There are times I feel like I'm a volcano that's ready to blow up from the inside out. Have you ever felt like a volcano? What happened to make you feel like erupting?"* Sparky takes a few minutes to listen to students' comments about a time when they were very angry and what caused them to feel that way.

Sparky then says: *"You know what? It's normal to feel angry like a volcano sometimes. Everybody gets angry. The important thing is what you do with your anger so you don't explode on someone else. If you're not careful, your anger can make somebody else feel like they need to erupt also and pretty soon everyone feels just like you did. Sometimes I need to count to 10. I do this to myself to help me calm down. One, two, three, four, five, six, seven, eight, nine, ten. Whew! I feel better. Here's another secret: It's called an I Message. Here's how it works. Suppose you're walking in the hall and someone trips you. How do you feel?"* Students label the emotion "angry" or "mad." *"Right! So tell the person it makes you mad. Here's how...take a minute and calm down...look the person in the eye and start your message with the word I."* Display the poster to the students. (*Note:* With younger students, cover the third component, "and I want you to...," with a piece of paper.) Sparky says: *"Here's the code"*:

"I feel...when you...and I want..."

"All you need to do is fill in the spaces and tell the other person how you feel."

"I feel **mad.**"

"Now tell them what he/she did to make you feel that way."

"I feel mad **when you pushed me down.**"

(*Note:* Stop here for younger students. For older students you may add the last component.)

"Now tell the person what you want them to do."

"I feel mad when you pushed me down **and I want you to stop.**"

Finally, remind students that any time you ask someone to do something, it's always nice to add "please." Encourage students to think of other incidents among peers that generally cause feelings of anger. Invite students to discuss how they usually handle these situations. Then point out that there are other ways to handle the "aggressor" without taking the situation to a new level. One way is to send I Messages. Examples of situations may include:

- You've been waiting a long time in the cafeteria line when someone cuts in ahead of you.
- You see a student across from you copying all the answers from your test.
- You see a student take your pencil and then walk away.
- Someone makes fun of you and calls you a name.
- Someone is spreading rumors about you that aren't true.
- Someone grabs the ball and runs away with it when you and your classmates are playing a game.

Role Playing I Messages PM68

Purpose: Role playing differs from both acting out stories and creative dramatics in that it requires children to think of and act out solutions to problems and to evaluate the solutions. Role playing is a valuable tool for helping children put themselves in another's place and for helping them make decisions.

Procedure: The following suggestions will help you use role playing in the classroom effectively:

- Wait until the class members are acquainted and at ease with one another before you introduce role playing.

- Anticipate some self-consciousness (evidenced, perhaps, by giggling and silliness) when you first introduce role playing. Tell the children that you felt awkward the first time you role played, too. Then remind them that the purpose of the activity is to practice using the I Message formula so they can see how it works.

- Have the students first role play the situation in a structured session with you guiding them. When students are comfortable with the format, ask them to do the same tasks in pairs.

- Ease their discomfort in the beginning by role playing a few of the ideas yourself and by demonstrating role-playing techniques. Sparky can role play with you to show students the format.

- Caution children not to hurt one another. Young children often become highly active in role-playing situations.

- Involve the children who are observing the role playing by urging them to listen carefully and to ask themselves, "What would I do?" and "Is there another way to solve this problem?"

- When an impasse occurs, discontinue the role play and ask if anyone else has an idea he or she wants to try out.

- Conclude the role playing by helping the children to evaluate their solutions. Ask, "Which solution do you think was the most effective?," "Why?," "What would you have said?," or "Has this ever happened to you?"

Follow-up Activity: Have students role play a few of the following incidents using the I Message sequence. Assign one student the role of the "problem situation" and the other student the role of the "I Message giver." Keep the I Message poster visible so children can refer to it. The pair can exchange roles at the conclusion of their session and role play the other character:

- A classmate breaks your lego construction.
- A classmate borrows your library book. When she returns it, several pages are torn.
- Someone tells you that you can't play kickball with him or her.
- You're waiting in line for the swings and someone cuts in front of you.
- A classmate grabs your coat from you.
- Someone pushes you in the hallway.
- A classmate tells you, "You're stupid."
- Someone walks by and scribbles on your paper.
- A classmate takes part of your lunch without asking you.
- Someone pulls your hair.
- A classmate takes part of your lunch without asking you.
- A classmate kicks your ball when you're playing with it.

Note: Students can use the Sparky Stick Puppets from PM50 during the role playing.

Formulating I Messages   PM69

Purpose: To provide opportunities for students to practice sending I Messages.

Materials:
- Sparky Puppet (PM 1).
- I Message poster (PM 67); enlarged to poster size for hanging.
- I Message form (PM 69); one per student duplicated on light-colored paper.
- Crayons, scissors, paste or glue stick (per student).

Procedure: Begin by briefly reviewing the steps to sending I Messages on the I Message poster. Sparky explains that I Messages are a wonderful way to be a peacemaker *"because you can calmly tell someone what is bothering you in a peaceful way."* Sparky asks students to think of a time they felt angry, bothered or frustrated. Emphasize that maybe the incident made them feel embarrassed or scared. Sparky says: *"Close your eyes and think about the problem. It may have happened today or a long time ago. What was the problem? How did you feel and what did you want to happen? One way you could have peacefully let the other person know how you felt was to use an I Message."* Students can then turn to a partner and tell about the experience. With younger children, you may wish to structure the activity by dividing it into three parts: first, students tell a partner a problem; second, they verbalize how they felt; and third, they express what they wanted to happen instead.

Distribute the I Message form to students and ask them to cut out the large "I" shape on the left side of the page. Next, have them cut out the facial expression that best shows how they felt about the problem. The feeling is glued in the dotted space next to the words "I feel." In the second space, students draw what made them feel that way. Finally, in the last space they depict what they wanted to have happened instead.

Tell students to sign their completed I Message. Depending on the level of security in students, they may share the I Mesage with the group, their partner, or alone to Sparky.

Extension Activity: Keep an ample supply of I Message forms available for students. These can be placed in a box somewhere handy in the classroom. Encourage students to use the form each time they have a problem that could use an I Message. For students capable of writing, you might duplicate extra copies of the I Message poster. Students can write their I Message on this form instead of drawing their responses.

Problems and Solutions   PM70

Purpose: To provide the opportunity for students to identify their problems and generate their own solutions.

Materials: Picture Problem/Solution Report (PM 70); an ample supply stored in a box or folder in a convenient location; crayons or marking pens.

Procedure: Inform the class that many times students report to staff members problems they could have solved themselves. These relatively insignificant problems take up staff time and lead to ill feelings among classmates because most often this kind of reporting is just "tattling." Tell the class that from now on, there is to be no reporting unless there is an injury (or likelihood of one happening) or the student really can't resolve it himself/herself.

This is the function of the report form: students draw pictures or write words describing their problems and turn the report into you. Let them know that you will make time to read the entire report. You will then decide if the case still warrants a conference. Encourage students to solve their own problems by drawing or writing a solution on the bottom half of the form.

What Would the Character Say? PM71

Purpose: To help students practice the technique of using the I Message formula.

Materials: Choose one of the recommended literature selections below or another book that portrays a character faced with the emotions of anger and frustration. Sparky Stick Puppets from PM 50 can be used for role playing by half of the students. The other half of the students need stick puppets representing the main character in the read aloud (the character faced with the problem). Copy a picture of the character from an illustration in the book, cut it out, and tape it on a popsicle stick, tongue depressor, straw, or ruler.

Procedure: Read the book aloud to students. As you come to the problem the character is faced with, stop the story *before the problem is solved.* Sparky stops and asks the students, " (Character's name) *is having a problem. Who can tell us what the problem is?"* Briefly discuss with the students what the problem is. Sparky then tells the class, *"Let's see if we can help this character get out of the terrible mess he/she is in."* You may wish to include specifics from the story here. *"I bet an I Message would work. He/she could let the other characters know how he/she feels. Let's try it. Who remembers how the I Message formula goes?"* Ask a few children to explain the formula. *"Right! Now what could the character say in an I Message that would help him/her?"* Help the children formulate the parts of the I Message formula for the character, then continue reading the book until the end.

At the conclusion of the reading, ask each student to find a partner. Distribute one Sparkle Puppet and one character puppet to each pair. Tell one student to pretend to be the character in the book who has the problem. The other student plays the role of Sparky helping the character to use the I Message formula to solve the problem.

Literature Suggestions: The following books are provided as catalysts for discussions dealing with conflict. As you read the book out loud to students, ask them how the characters might have used the I Message formula to solve their problems.

Angel Child, Dragon Child by Michele Maria Surat (Scholastic, 1983). Ut has just come to the United States from Vietnam, and she does not like her new American school. She is taunted by her classmates for her differences (especially by one red-haired boy). The principal finds the perfect way to help them resolve their differences.

I'll Fix Anthony by Judith Viorst (Harper, 1969). What every child feels and plans while being plagued by an older brother or sister is dramatized in this book.

No Fighting, No Biting! by Else Holmelund Minarik (Harper, 1978). This is the story of a squabbling little brother and sister who can't refrain from their constant rivalry.

The Temper Tantrum Book by Edna Mitchell Preston (Viking Press, 1969). Bothering, annoying, roaring, infuriating, and frustrating situations are humorously portrayed by animal characters.

Norma Jean, Jumping Bean by Joanna Cole (Random House, 1987). Norma Jean, a kangaroo whose love of jumping might be a bit excessive, stops her favorite activity of jumping after her friends complain.

Nobody Listens to Andrew by Elizabeth Guilfoile (Scholastic, 1967). A classic story of a little boy named Andrew with a major problem and his dilemma that no one will listen to him.

The Shrinking of Treehorn by Florence Parry Heide (Holiday House, 1971). When a young boy mentions to his parents that he's begun to shrink, he's ignored. When he calls it to the attention of his teachers, his words fall on deaf ears. Day by day he grows smaller, and day by day the adults continue to talk about him and his problem.

Harry and the Terrible Whatzit by Dick Gackenbach (Scholastic, 1977). When his mother doesn't return immediately from her errand in the cellar, little Harry is positive she's been captured by the monsters he thinks live down there. Harry finally confronts the Whatzit to solve the problem.

Fat, Fat Rose Marie by Lisa Passen (Henry Holt and Co., 1991). A little girl must stand up to the class bully who keeps picking on her overweight friend.

The Hating Book by Charlotte Zolotow (Harper & Row, 1969). This book by a much esteemed children's writer has become a classic for reducing conflicts. In this tale of two friends who hate one another, things will never be right again until they decide to talk to one another.

Our Planet of Delight Mural   PM72

Purpose: To help students express how the four Sparky character building concepts could create a more peaceful community.

Materials:
• Eye/Ear/Heart Patterns (PM 14a, 14b, 14c).

- Two or three large mural papers (one piece for each group of 10 to 12 students).
- Pastel chalk, colored markers, crayons, paint, and brushes.
- Sparky Puppet.

Procedure: Sparky asks students to imagine what the world would look like if everyone did and said Sparkles to light up other people on the inside. He says, *"Close your eyes and picture your classroom, school, family, and neighborhood. Imagine a place, like the Planet of Delight, where everyone gets along and everyone has happy faces. There is no fighting. Everyone is using the lessons we learned. What are the people doing to show their peacefulness toward one another? What are they saying? How does the sender of Sparkles feel? How does the receiver of Sparkles feel?…Now open your eyes. What did you see?"*

On a piece of paper or chalkboard, write the caption: "Our Planet of Delight." Make a large T-chart and tape the eye, ear and heart patterns onto the board to represent the three columns as pictured below. Fill in the chart with the sights, sounds, and emotions of peacefulness as students describe them.

OUR PLANET OF DELIGHT

Looks Like	Sounds Like	Feels Like

Now divide the students into groups of ten or twelve (or smaller). Distribute mural paper and drawing materials to each group. Sparky explains that each person is to express their idea of what a Planet of Delight could look like on earth. Emphasize that the mural is to be a peacemaking activity. Sparky is looking for students who are Sparky pals. At the conclusion of the activity, hang up the murals and ask individual students to describe to

Sparky what their contribution to the mural was and what a Planet of Delight means to them.

Sparky Ambassadors PM73

Purpose: To review the four positive attitude and peacemaking concepts with students: 1. increasing positive comments and deeds; 2. deflecting negative comments; 3. accepting compliments; and 4. using I Messages to resolve conflicts and to convey to students the importance of transferring these concepts to their everyday lives.

Materials: Sparky Ambassador Certificate (PM 73); one per student. Teacher uses Sparky Puppet.

Sparky Says Goodbye

Sparky says: *"It sure has been fun working together with all of you. We've come a long way since the day the Planet of Doom was threatened with extinction. The kinds of things we've learned and worked on helped save the planet and turn it into the Planet of Delight."* (*Note:* In Sparky's farewell to the students, describe the Mural of the Planet of Delight the students did in the previous session.) *"Just four simple ideas helped bring this about. One, we learned how to use positive statements called Sparkles and to back up these words with positive actions or deeds. Two, we found out that negative statements are called Stingers and how we can put an end to them so no one gets hurt. Third, we practiced accepting compliments by looking people in the eye, smiling, and saying 'thank you.' Finally, we learned how to put together an I Message that can help us solve problems and resolve conflicts."*

Sparky continues, *"The most important thing I want you to learn is that we need to do more than make our classroom, or even our school, shine. We need to make the whole earth a more delightful and peaceful place to live. Wherever we go, we'll find people who need to be lighted up and who need to learn the lessons you've been taught in this classroom. When you take what you've learned in this classroom out into the world, you'll be what's called an ambassador. An ambassador is someone who represents his or her country. He leaves his own country and goes to another country to create good feelings between the two of them. He is a messenger of peace. That's what you'll be doing once you leave this classroom with the ideas that were first learned on the Planet of Delight. You'll be helping to create more peace and togetherness in the world. You'll be making other people feel good about themselves and about you. As a Sparky Ambassador, you have the power to take the skills you've learned and light up the world with Sparkles."*

Literature Suggestions: The following literature suggestions are wonderful additions to any classroom library. Each book beautifully describes the concept of peace in language children can understand.

 Peace Begins With You by Katherine Scholes (Sierra Club Books, 1989). In simple terms, the book explains the concept of peace, why conflicts occur, how they can be resolved in positive ways, and how to promote peace.

 Secret of the Peaceful Warrior by Dan Milman (H.J. Kramer, Inc. 1992). An old man named Socrates shows Dan that the best way of dealing with a bully is the way of the peaceful warrior: through courage and love.

 The Three Astronauts by Umberto Eco and Eugenio Carmi (Harcourt Brace Jovanovich, 1989). In this gem for all ages, three astronauts from different countries land on Mars, meet a strange Martian, and make an amazing discovery about the nature of humanity.

The Tale of the Vanishing Rainbow by Siegfried P. Rupprecht (Northsouth Books, 1989). This simple, eloquent tale teaches children an important lesson in cooperation and defusing conflict.

  The Great Peace March by Holly Nera (Henry Holt & Co., 1993). An illustrated version of a powerful song celebrating the brotherhood of humanity and the possibility of world peace.

 The Big Book of Peace edited by Ann Durell and Marilyn Sachs (Dutton, 1990). A special volume on peace created by more than thirty of the best-known and loved children's authors and illustrators. Filled with stories, pictures, poems, and even a song, the book clearly emphasizes the wisdom of peace and the absurdity of fighting.

 Happy Birthday, Martin Luther King by Jean Marzollo (Scholastic, 1993). Here is a beautiful introduction to a great civil rights leader written for young children. The book's rich and spirited illustrations help capture the magic of a real American hero.

Puppets

Please refer to pages 15-18,
"How to use Character Builder Puppets,"
for ways to use the puppet images.

Permission to reprint for classroom use,
Character Builders, Jalmar Press
© 2001 by Michele Borba

SPARKY

STINGER

Worksheets, Activities, and Posters

Name _____ Date _____

Sparkle Statements

You're cool.
Let's play together.
I like knowing you.
You look nice today.
You're a good friend.
Can we work together?
It's fun knowing you.
It's great working with you.
I'd like to know you better.
I like your outfit.
Thanks for being you.
Thanks for being such a buddy.
You're really good at _____.
I like it when you _____.
Thank you for _____.
I like sharing with you.
Can we sit together.
Can I share with you?
I'm proud to know you.
I'm glad you're here today.
I like your smile.
You brighten my day.
You're my special friend.
Thanks for sharing yourself.
I'm glad we're buddies.
Hello!
Hi!
I enjoy you.
Thank you!
You contribute good things.
Thanks for your kindness.
I hope you do well.
I hope we're together today.
Have a good one.
Let's help each other.
You were helpful when you _____.

I especially appreciated it when you

_____ .
You're fun to be with.
Congratulations on your _____.
You're clothes look rad!
I feel good when I'm with you.
I'm proud of you.
You make me happy.
Will you be my friend?
Thanks for listening.
You're great.
I like you!
It's good to see you.
I like to sit by you.
You're a good team member.
Have a good day.
Will you play with me?
You're special.
I like to be with you.
You're a good buddy.
Good morning!
I like your _____.
I'm glad I know you.
Let's get to know each other better.
I'm lucky to know you.
You're my friend.
Thanks for your support.
Hope today is super for you.
Good luck today.
I like the way you _____.
I hope today is great for you.
I appreciate you.
I look forward to seeing you.
I'm glad we're on the same team.
You deserve a pat on the back for

_____ .

Name _____ Date _____

Making a Smile Book

1. Look through magazines. Find pictures of people who have great smiles. Cut out the smiles and paste them on the cover of your book. Now look at the cover. How does it make you feel?

2. At home, look at old photographs of your self. Find one that shows you with a great smile. Bring it to school with you and glue it in your book on page 2. Write about things that make you smile on page 3.

3. Find three friends. Measure the length of each of their smiles. Write your findings on pages 4 and 5 of your book.
1. Who are your friends?
2. What are the lengths of your friends' smiles?
3. What are the widths of your friends' smiles?

4. Read through the newspaper. Find a story that makes you smile. Cut it out and paste it in your book. What made you choose the story? What was it about it made you smile? Write your reasons on pages 6-7.

Boy   Girl   Male   Female

5. Make a survey of people in your school whom *you* think have great smiles. Find a smile winner for each category: boy, girl, adult male and adult female. Write your answer on pages 8 and 9. What was special about each winner's smile?

OUT

IN

MY
SMILE
FILE

Nice Things to Say

My Ideas:

Hi
Hello!
I like you.
How are you?
You're a good friend.
You look nice today.
Let's be friends!
You're nice.
I'm glad I know you.
Thanks for helping me.
You're special.
Can I help you?

(Fold up)

(Fold up)

A Sparkle to: _____

From: _____

Message: _____

A Sparkle to: _____

From: _____

Message: _____

A Sparkle to: _____

From: _____

Message: _____

A Sparkle to: _____

From: _____

Message: _____

Sparkle Boy and Girl

Girl
Pattern

Boy
Pattern

Sparkle Book Cover

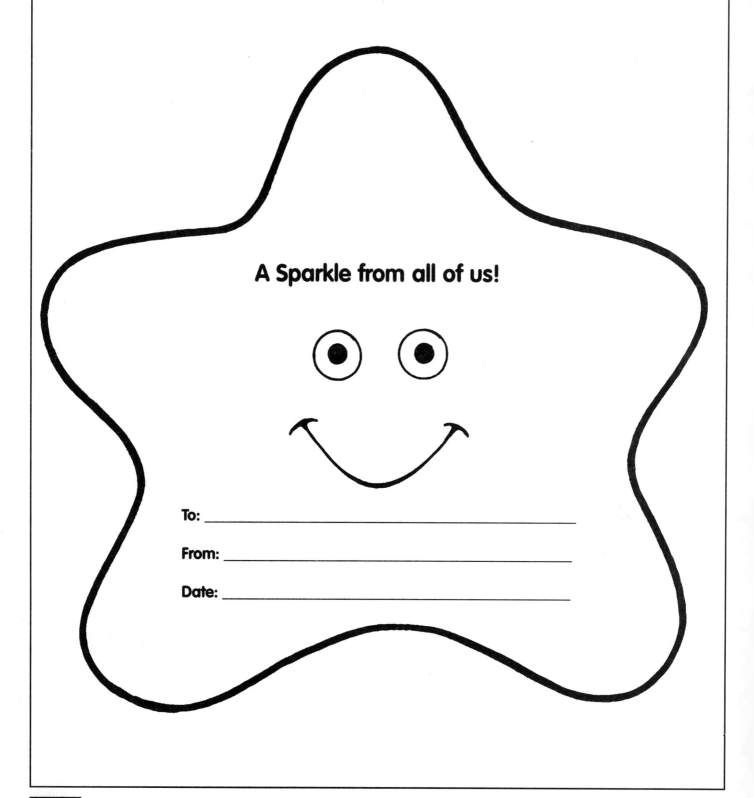

A Sparkle from all of us!

To: _____

From: _____

Date: _____

A Month of Positive Attitudes
Draw or write what positive things you did each day.

Monday	Tuesday	Wednesday	Thursday	Friday

PM11

Name _____ **Date** _____

Happy Happenings

Monday

Tuesday

Wednesday

Thursday

Friday

PM14a

SOUNDS LIKE

FEELS LIKE

POSITIVE ATTITUDES

YES! I KNEW YOU COULD. GIVE IT A SHOT. YOU CAN IF YOU TRY. IT'S ALL ATTITUDE.

AWESOME. YES! I KNEW YOU COULD. GIVE IT A SHOT. YOU CAN IF YOU TRY. IT'S ALL ATTITUDE. THINK POSITIVE. KEEP IT UP. AWESOME.

GIVE IT A TRY. THINK POSITIVE. RADICAL. DON'T WORRY · THINK POSITIVE. TRY YOUR HARDEST. KEEP IT UP.

COOL! YOU CAN IF YOU TRY. GIVE IT A SHOT. IT'S ALL ATTITUDE. THINK POSITIVE.

"Seeing the bright side of things.
Meeting life in an upbeat and cheerful manner."

· AWESOME. JUST TRY YOUR BEST. I LIKE IT. SUPER! TRY THINKING POSITIVE.

PM14d

PM15b

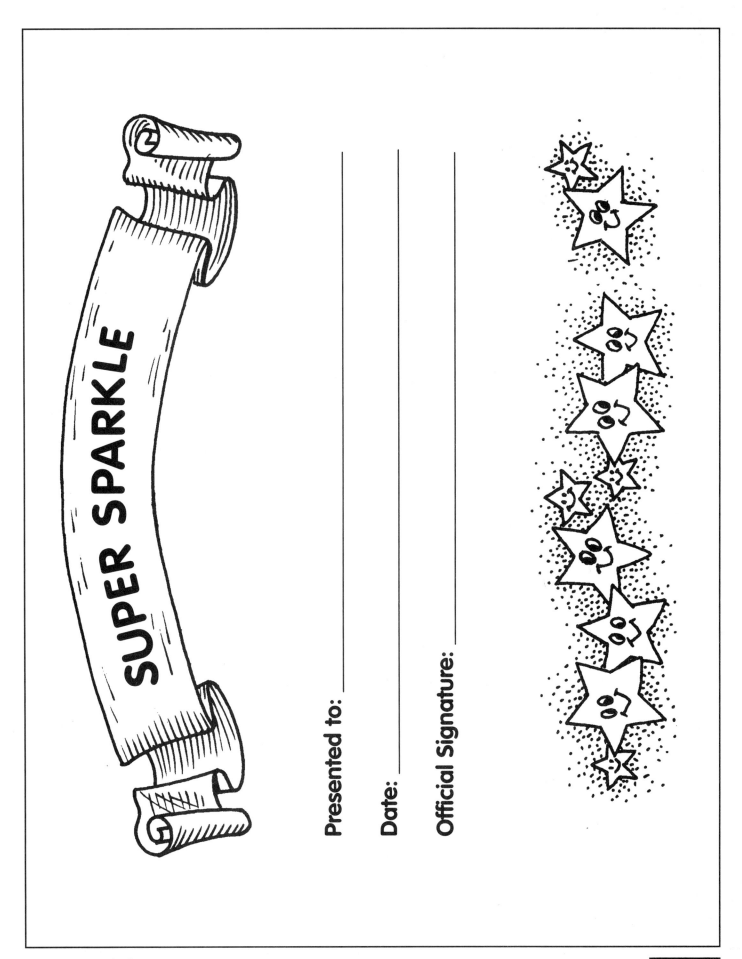

SUPER SPARKLE

Presented to: _____

Date: _____

Official Signature: _____

PM19a

Positive Performers

I saw _____ performing
a positive deed today.

The deed was _____
_____
_____

Signed: _____ Date: _____

Positive Performers

I saw _____ performing
a positive deed today.

The deed was _____
_____
_____

Signed: _____ Date: _____

Positive Performers

I saw _____ performing
a positive deed today.

The deed was _____
_____
_____

Signed: _____ Date: _____

PM19b

Permission to reprint for classroom use.
Character Builders, Jalmar Press
© 2001 by Michele Borba

Positive Performance Award

POSITIVE PERFORMANCE

_____

was caught
being positive.

We liked it!

AWARD

POSITIVE PERFORMANCE

_____

was caught
being positive.

We liked it!

AWARD

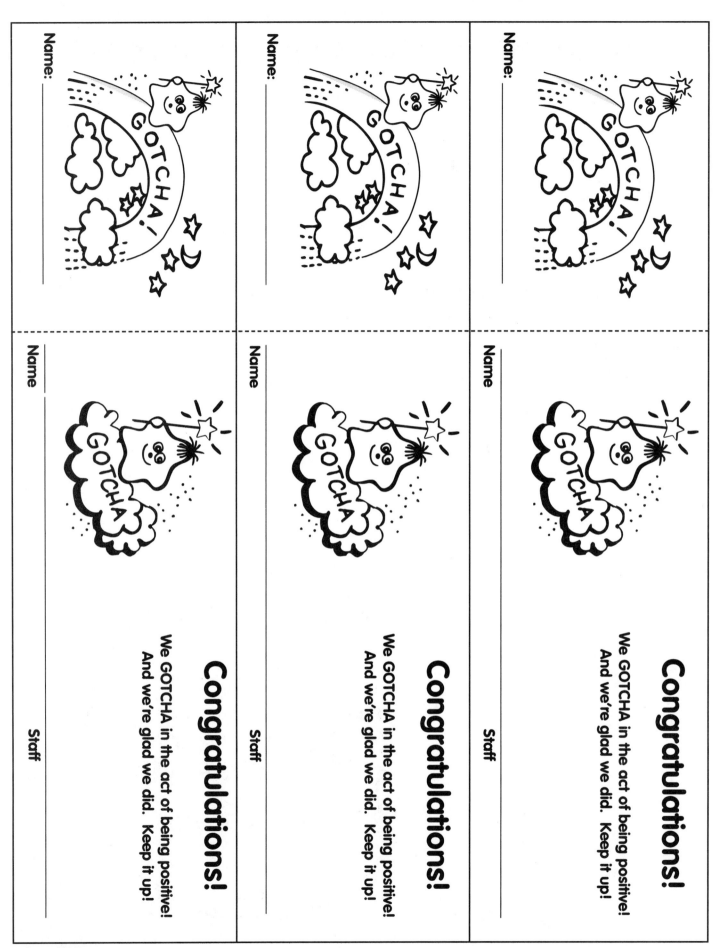

Name: _____

GOTCHA!

Name: _____

GOTCHA!

Name _____

GOTCHA!

Name _____

GOTCHA

Staff _____

Congratulations!

We GOTCHA in the act of being positive!
And we're glad we did. Keep it up!

Name _____

GOTCHA

Staff _____

Congratulations!

We GOTCHA in the act of being positive!
And we're glad we did. Keep it up!

Name _____

GOTCHA

Staff _____

Congratulations!

We GOTCHA in the act of being positive!
And we're glad we did. Keep it up!

Sparky, Sparky,
  We love you.
You help us sparkle.
  Yes, you do.

Your Sparkles make us
  Shine so bright.
Our classroom now
  is full of light.

Sparky, Sparky,
  We love you.
You help us sparkle.
  Yes, you do.

(Sung to the tune of
"Twinkle Twinkle Little Star")

ACCEPTING COMPLIMENTS

1. I look 'em in the eye

2. This is the first thing I do

3. Then I put on a smile

4. And say... "thank you!"

PM25

Recording Sparky Deeds

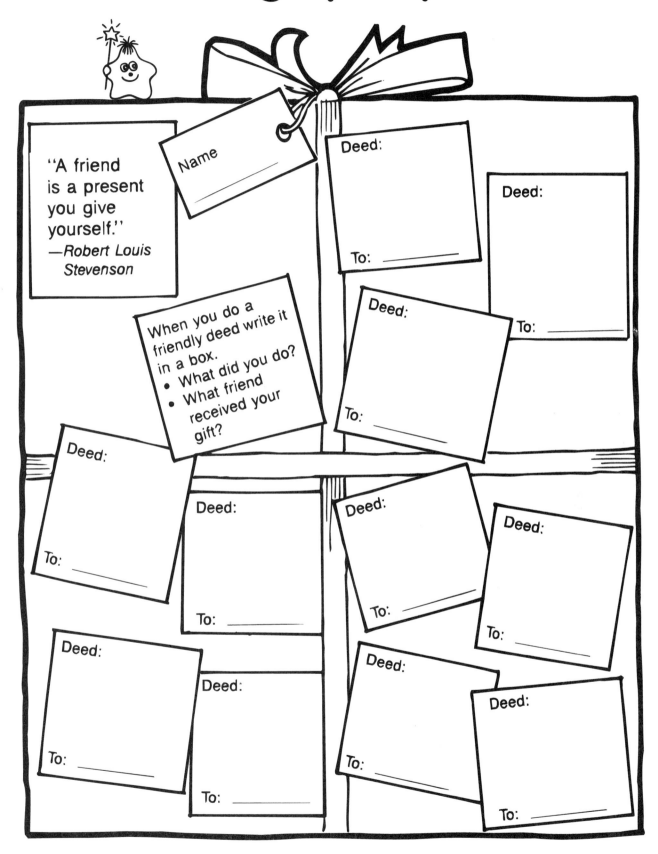

"A friend is a present you give yourself."
—Robert Louis Stevenson

Name _____

When you do a friendly deed write it in a box.
• What did you do?
• What friend received your gift?

Deed:

To: _____

Deed:

To: _____

Deed:

To: _____

Deed:

To: _____

Deed:

To: _____

Deed:

To: _____

Deed:

To: _____

Deed:

To: _____

Deed:

To: _____

Deed:

To: _____

Compliment Hanging

O

A Compliment to:

_____

From:

_____

Compliment:

_____

O

O

A Compliment to:

_____

From:

_____

Compliment:

_____

O

O

A Compliment to:

_____

From:

_____

Compliment:

_____

O

PM31a

Permission to reprint for classroom use.
Character Builders, Jalmar Press
© 2001 by Michele Borba

Compliment Hanging

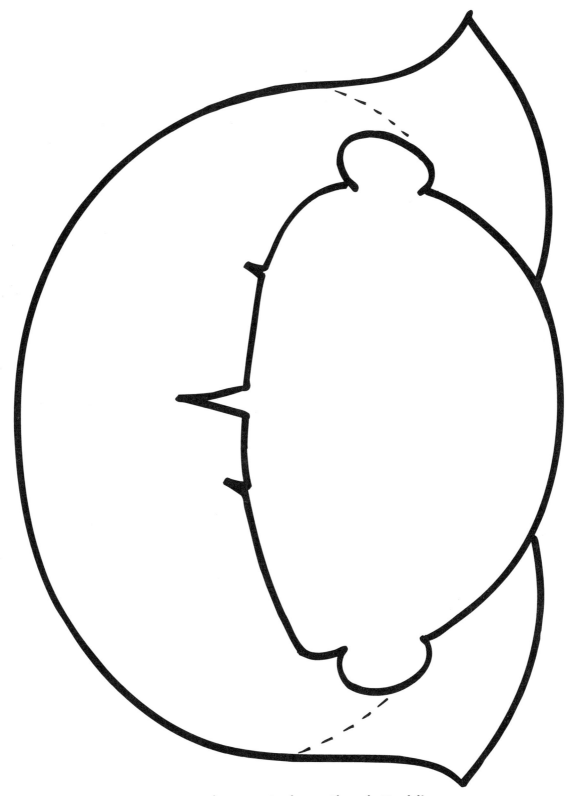

To represent a boy, cut along the dotted lines.

Dictionary
of Feelings

Author _____

Copyright _____

Pictures of others feeling this way:

Silly

How I Look:

A time I felt this way was . . .

_____

_____

_____

_____

_____

1

14

Pictures of others feeling this way:

Angry

How I Look:

A time I felt this way was . . .

_____

_____

_____

_____

_____

_____

13

2

Pictures of others feeling this way:

Scared

How I Look:

A time I felt this way was . . .

_____

_____

_____

_____

_____

_____

3

12

PM56

Pictures of others feeling this way:

Happy

How I Look:

A time I felt this way was . . .

_____

_____

_____

_____

_____

11

4

Pictures of others feeling this way:

Sad

How I Look:

A time I felt this way was . . .

_____

_____

_____

_____

_____

_____

5

10

Pictures of others feeling this way:

Lonely

How I Look:

A time I felt this way was . . .

_____

_____

_____

_____

_____

_____

9

6

Permission to reprint for classroom use.
Character Builders, Jalmar Press
© 2001 by Michele Borba

Pictures of others feeling this way:

Proud

How I Look:

A time I felt this way was . . .

_____

_____

_____

_____

_____

_____

7

8

Feelings Wheel

How I Feel Wheel

by

_____

Feelings Wheel

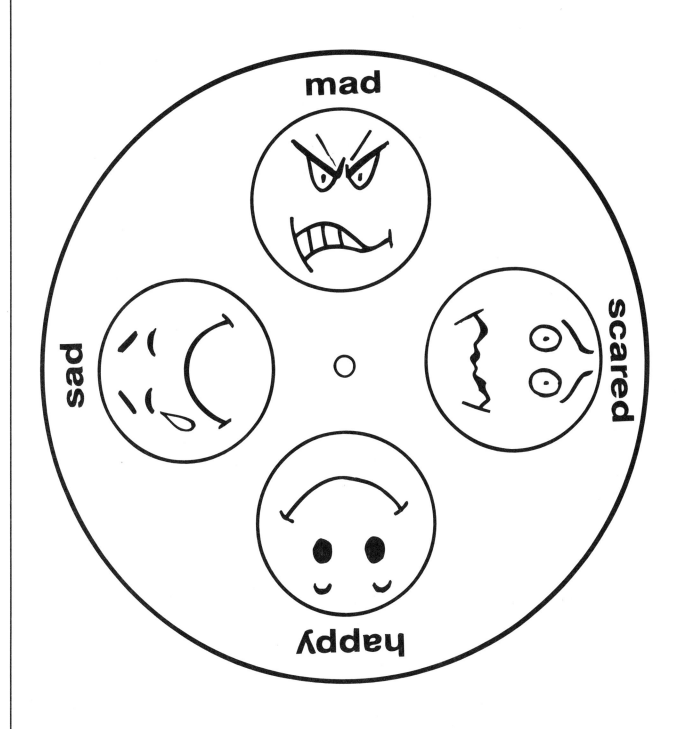

PM57

I Feel . . . You Feel

I feel _____ and
you feel _____ .

I guess everyone has a different
view.

That's what makes me . . . me,
and you . . . you!

"I" MESSAGES

SMILE. PRAISE OTHERS.· USE "I" MESSAGES. NO PUT DOWNS. DON'T INTERRUPT. LISTEN RESPECTFULLY. USE YOUR WORDS.

SOLVE PROBLEMS COOLY. ACT CALMLY. NO PUT DOWNS. SAY "THANK YOU." USE POSITIVE LANGUAGE. SMILE

1. I feel _____

HAPPY   SAD   ANGRY   SCARED   FRUSTRATED   EMBARRASSED

+

2. when you _____

+

3. and I want you to _____

_____.

I FEEL MAD WHEN YOU GRAB MY PENCILS.

THANKS FOR TELLING ME HOW YOU FEEL.

MESSAGES

1, 2, 3, 4, 5, 6, 7, 8, 9, 10
Calm down

1. I feel

+

2. when you

+

3. and I want you to

HAPPY

SAD

SCARED

FRUSTRATED

EMBARRASSED

Picture Problem/Solution Report

Draw a picture of what happened.

Draw a picture of how you could have solved it.

SPARKY AMBASSADOR AWARD

Awarded to: _____

Date: _____

Presented by _____

(name of teacher)

For completing the Character Builders Program in positive attitude and peacemaking.

Using Sparkle Statements   **Combatting Stingers**   **Using I-Messages**   **Accepting Compliments**

STAYING CALM

1 + 3 + 10 = Calm

1 **Tell yourself: "Be calm!"**

+

3 **Slowly take 3 deep breaths.**

+

1 2 3

10 **Count slowly to 10.**

I can act responsibly by staying calm.

Join Over a Half a Million Teachers and Parents for a Workshop by Dr. Borba
• Effective Teaching • Character Building • Parenting • Esteem Building • Moral Intelligence

Dr. Michele Borba's sessions are entertaining and enlightening, always provide real-life examples and proven solutions, and are guaranteed to change the way you deal with kids. Michele does keynote presentations, half-day, full-day, two-day and week-long training programs for your staff development and community training desires.

* You Are The Door Opener: A Keynote Address for Educators
This motivating and inspiring keynote explains why educators do have the power to impact their students' lives and help them reach their potential as learners. Using inspiring stories and real-life examples of teachers who are making a difference, educators are reminded they are door openers to a students' future because they offer five critical keys that maximize their students' success.

* Character Builders: How to Teach the Traits of Solid Character
Would you like your students to be more responsible and respectful? Then here's the program for you! Literally dozens of ways to enhance student character development are offered with a special emphasis on how to help students learn solid character behaviors and be more respectful and responsible. Monthly character themes that can be incorporated school-wide as well as in the classroom will also be shared and all ideas can be instantly integrated into subject content. Based on Dr. Borba's *Character Builders* program.

* Helping All Students Succeed: What Works!
The best teaching practices proven to help students learn more, behave better, be more engaged in their learning, and develop greater responsibility. While ALL students will benefit from the highly useful strategies shared, those with the most difficulties succeeding will especially benefit. Dozens of active learning techniques and quick processors to increase retention and nurture learning success are offered and all can enhance any subject at any grade level.

* Strengthening At-Risk Students' Achievement and Behavior
This seminar shares strategies for identifying high-risk students, and a wealth of proven techniques for strengthening their achievement, self-control, and motivation. Participants leave with dozens of practical strategies to help rebuild a cycle of success for our defeated youth that they can begin using tomorrow!

* Parents Do Make A Difference: A Special Parent Address
Parents learn practical ways to teach their children the eight critical traits of success: positive self-esteem, communicating, cultivating strengths, teamwork, problem-solving, goal-setting, perseverance, and caring. Practical ways to raise kids with solid character, strong minds and caring hearts are shared. Based on Dr. Borba's book *Parents do Make A Difference*.

* Esteem Building: Increasing Achievement, Behavior and Learning Climates
Practical strategies for identifying and helping low esteem students and a model for esteem-building based on the five building blocks identified in Dr. Borba's best-selling book, *Esteem Builders*. Dozens of classroom-proven techniques and activities to strengthen their classroom environment to enhance students' self esteem and in the process improve their students' behavior and achievement are offered.

* Building Moral Intelligence: Our Last Best Hope
Moral intelligence is the growing capacity to decipher right from wrong, choose what's right then behave morally and teaching it may be our best hope for preventing peer cruelty, violence, and anti-social behaviors. This session explores the latest research that confirms how teaching moral intelligence can enhance our students' prosocial behaviors and replace negative ones and provides practical strategies that can easily be implemented in any program that teach students the essential moral behaviors of empathy, conscience, self-control, respect, kindness, tolerance, and fairness. Based on Dr. Borba's latest book, *Building Moral Intelligence*.

**Contact Dr. Borba at Office/fax (760)323-5387 • E-mail BorbaM@aol.com
A complete list of sessions is available on Dr. Borba's website: www.Moralintelligence.com**

(left margin, vertical text) Coping with Trauma • Character Development • Problem Solving Skills • Social Competence • Positive School Climate • Conflict Resolution Skills •

(right margin, vertical text) • self-concept • **AFFILIATION** - belonging and connectedness • **MISSION** - purpose and responsibility • **COMPETENCE** - capableness and self-efficacy •

ESTEEM BUILDERS COMPLETE PROGRAM
By Dr. Michele Borba

A comprehensive K-8 program for educators, students, and parents to improve achievement, behavior, and school climate.

Research has validated that Self-Esteem is a KEY factor in improving student behavior and academic achievement. Educators recognize the urgency of these findings and are asking themselves,

"How do we enhance the self-esteem of our students?"

The Esteem Builders' Complete Program
provides the answer.

• Program is based on the recognition that everyone—home, school, and community—must be involved.
• Each program component works together to ensure a successful esteem building program and to build student self-esteem with special attention to "at risk" students.
• Prevention approach to many of the challenges effecting students when low self-esteem is present: substance abuse, gangs, behavior problems, school dropouts, and under-achievement.

Unique Benefits

• **Helps all students** —"at-risk", special education, new and existing students —at school, in the home, and in the community.
• **One stop source** — eight components and the over 1,200 activities to service students and all school personnel.
• **It works** — founded on over 10 years of researched and field-tested esteem building strategies.
• **Based on the 5 building blocks** — self-esteem: security, selfhood, affiliation, mission, and competence.
• **Easy to use** — student activites cross-correlated to both grade level and curriculum content.

Esteem Builder Pilot Site Study Results

One of the most comprehensive studies on the impact of implementing a self-esteem schoolwide program has just been released. The study was conducted to detemine the effectiveness of using the self-esteem program, *Esteem Builders*, on elementary students' behavior and academic self-concept. The program was implemented over a one-year school period on 1,040 K-6 grade students at three diverse public school sites with high at-risk populations: Brooklyn Park, MN, Surrey, BC and Hays, KS. Both qualitative and quantitative measures were used to determine program aggression reports and a norm-referenced instrument assessing self-concept behaviors.
Study results using the *Esteem Builders* Program shows:
• **decrease in physical (41%) and verbal (39%) aggression**
• **increase in prosocial behaviors (90% of general school climate is more positive)**
• **increase in students' academic self-concept**
• **lower aggressive behavior particularly for at risk youth.**

For a summary report, please contact Jalmar Press.

Program Components

• Teacher's Guide: **ESTEEM BUILDERS**: A K-8 curriculum for Improving Student Achievement, Behavior and School Climate. Contains over 250-theory based and field-tested esteem building activities cross-correlated to all subject areas and grade levels, making it possible to include self-esteem activities in the current curriculum, every minute of every day.
JP9053 paperback $39.95   JP9088 spiral $49.95
• **STAFF ESTEEM BUILDERS**. The administrator's bible for enhancing staff self-esteem.   *JP9804 $44.95*
• **HOME ESTEEM BUILDERS**. Vignette sessions provides a variety of activities designed to strengthen the partnership between home and school and to help parents in their home esteem building endeavors.
JP9065 $34.95
• **RESOURCES FOR THE EBCP**. Compendium of self-esteem resources including research & statistics, a bibliography, agency and organization listings, and an informal assessment listing. *JP9625 $34.95*
• **OVERVIEW OF EBCP**. Describes and indexes the major elements and their roles in the EBCP. Guidelines help administrators set up Esteem Building. *JP9600 $44.95*
• **TRAINER'S MANUAL**. Provides the trainer with materials, including blackline masters and participant handouts. Plus 15 hours of scripts for training the staff in esteem building. *JP9078 $129.95*
• **ESTEEM BUILDER POSTERS**. Eight posters featuring esteem building principles. *JP9605 $18.95*
• **AUDIO CASSETTES**. Dr. Borba leads the trainer and staff in an understanding of the five building blocks of self-esteem on six audio cassettes. *JP9622 $89.95*
• **EBCP Complete Program Kit**
Kit includes all components. *JP9086 $448.60*

To order call: (800)662-9662
Jalmar Press
P. O. Box 1185, Torrance, CA 90505
Fax: (310)816-3092 • E-mail: jalmarpress@att.net
Website: www.jalmarpress.com

ORDER FORM

Customer Service Hotline
(800)662-9662

Ordered by:
Name _____
School/Company_____
Address_____
City_____State___Zip_____

Ship to:
Name _____
School/Company_____
Address_____
City_____State___Zip_____

Check payment method used:
__ Check enclosed.   ___VISA   __MasterCard   ___Discover   __AMEX
Card Number _____ Exp. Date _____
Signature (as it appears on card) _____

Purchase order #_____
Please attach your purchase order to completed order form.

For fastest service call toll free (800)662-9662, 24 hours a day, 7 days a week!

MAIL OR FAX YOUR ORDER TO:
JALMAR PRESS
P. O. BOX 1185
TORRANCE, CA 90505
(310)816-3092

Character Builders	Order #	Price	Qty	Total
Responsibility and Trustworthiness	JP9654	$19.95	___	$____
Respect for Self and Others	JP9655	$19.95	___	$____
Fairness and Cooperation*	JP9656	$19.95	___	$____
Caring*	JP9658	$19.95	___	$____
Positive Attitudes and Peacemaking	JP9659	$19.95	___	$____

*Not available yet.

Each volume 200 pages, 8-1/2" x 11", filled with illustrations, posters and activities.

Esteem Builders' Complete Program	Order#	Price	Qty	Total
Esteem Builders, paperback	JP9053	$39.95	___	$____
Esteem Builders, spiral	JP9088	$49.95	___	$____
Staff Esteem Builders	JP9604	$44.95	___	$____
Home Esteem Builders	JP9065	$34.95	___	$____
Resources for EBCP	JP9625	$34.95	___	$____
Overview of EBCP	JP9600	$44.95	___	$____
Trainer's Manual	JP9078	$129.95	___	$____
Esteem Builders Posters	JP9605	$18.95	___	$____
Five Building Blocks, Audios	JP9622	$89.95	___	$____
EBCP Complete Program Kit	JP9086	$448.60	___	$____

Subtotal $_____
California residents add sales tax _____
Add 10% for shipping (minimum $5.00)_____
TOTAL$ _____

Order on the internet: www.jalmarpress.com or e-mail to: jalmarpress@att.net

Esteem Builder Research Results:

- **Decreases in Physical and Verbal Aggression and Detentions.**
- **Increases in Academic Self-Concept Behaviors.**
- **Increases in Prosocial Behaviors.**
- **Significant Gains in Low Self-Esteem Students.**

- **Decreases in Physical and Verbal Aggression and Detentions.**
  - **46% REDUCTION in Detention Incidences.**
  - **41% REDUCTION in Physical Aggression Incidences.**
  - **39% REDUCTION in Verbal Aggression Incidences.**

- **Increases in 11 Academic Self-Concept Behaviors:**
  - **Willingness to undertake new tasks.**
  - **Make decisions and establish goals.**
  - **Takes criticism or corrections in stride.**
  - **Company is sought by peers.**
  - **Acts as a leader in group situations.**
  - **Refers to self in genuinely positive terms.**
  - **Readily express opinions.**
  - **Self direction and independence in activities.**
  - **Initiates new ideas relative to classroom activities.**
  - **Ask questions when doesn't understand.**
  - **Comfortably deals with mistakes or failures.**

- **Increases in Prosocial Behaviors:** (Based on teacher responses at all three pilot schools).
  - **Students spoke more positively—100%**
  - **Students were more respectful and tolerant of each other—95%**
  - **Students were more caring and supportive of each other—93%**
  - **Students were more cooperative—93%**
  - **Students were more courteous—91%**
  - **Greater proficiency in friendship making skills—91%**
  - **Ability to solve problems and resolve conflict—89%**

- **Significant Gains in Low Self-Esteem Students.**
  - **Overall growth rate from 64-98%.**